PracticePM

A handy reference for project management practice using PMP approach

David London
3rd Edition

Copyright © 2018 by AITechConsulting

ISBN: Softcover   978-1729649954

All rights reserved. No part of this book may be reproduced or transmitted in any form or by any means, electronic or mechanical, including photocopying, recording, or by any information storage and retrieval system, without permission in writing from the copyright owner.

This book was printed in the United States of America.

To order additional copies of this book, contact:
AITechConsulting Ltd
+1800 561 02 63
businessdev@aitechconsulting.com

CONTENTS

DEDICATION 7

PREFACE 8

CHAPTER 1: PREPARING FOR PMP® EXAM 10

CHAPTER 2: ABOUT THE PMP® EXAM 12

CHAPTER 3: ON THE DAY OF THE EXAM 13

    TAKE THE FOLLOWING ITEMS WITH YOU TO THE EXAM CENTER: 13
    OTHER IDEAS THAT YOU SHOULD KEEP IN MIND TO AID IN PASSING PMP® EXAM: 13

CHAPTER 4: PROJECT 14

    WHAT IS A PROJECT? 14
    WHAT ARE THE DIFFERENCES BETWEEN PROJECT AND OPERATIONS? 15
    PROJECTS ARE FOR STRATEGIC ACHIEVEMENTS 16
    FACTORS THAT CONTRIBUTE TO SUCCESSFUL PROJECTS 16
    PORTFOLIO, PROGRAMS AND PROJECT 16
    ROLES OF PORTFOLIO, PROGRAM AND PROJECT MANAGERS 17
    PROJECT ENVIRONMENT 19
        Enterprise Environmental Factors *19*
        Organizational Process Assets *19*

CHAPTER 5: WHAT IS PROJECT MANAGEMENT? 20

    KNOWLEDGE AND SKILLS REQUIRED FOR PROJECT MANAGEMENT 20
    BUSINESS VALUE, PROJECT MANAGEMENT, OPERATIONS MANAGEMENT AND ORGANIZATION STRATEGY 23
    WHO IS A PROJECT MANAGER? 24

CHAPTER 6: WHAT IS PROJECT LIFE CYCLE? 27

    TYPES OF PROJECT LIFE CYCLE 30
    WHAT IS THE PROJECT PROCESS (OR LIFE CYCLE) IN YOUR ORGANIZATION? 32

CHAPTER 7: PROJECT STAKEHOLDERS AND ORGANIZATION 35

    WHO ARE THE PROJECT STAKEHOLDERS? 35
    ORGANIZATIONAL STRUCTURE AND PROJECT ORGANIZATION 36

What is the organizational structure for this project? *36*
What is the organizational framework? *37*
Organizational Structure *38*
What is the organizational culture? *42*
Other Supporting Systems and Office for Project Organization *43*

CHAPTER 8: WHAT IS PROJECT MANAGEMENT PROCESS? 44

Project Management Process versus Project Process *45*
Project Management: Level of Activity Chart (Time versus Effort) *46*
Why iterate project management process groups? *48*
Summary of Project Management Process *49*

CHAPTER 9: PLANNING A PROJECT FROM END TO END USING PMBOK® 50

PLANNING 53
EXECUTING 55
MONITORING AND CONTROLLING 56
CLOSING 58

CHAPTER 10: INTEGRATION MANAGEMENT 59

DEVELOP PROJECT CHARTER 59
DEVELOP PROJECT MANAGEMENT PLAN 61
DIRECT AND MANAGE PROJECT EXECUTION 63
MANAGE PROJECT KNOWLEDGE 63
MONITOR AND CONTROL PROJECT WORK 63
PERFORM INTEGRATED CHANGE CONTROL 63
CLOSE PROJECT OR PHASE 64

CHAPTER 11: PROJECT SCOPE MANAGEMENT 65

EXPECTED OUTPUTS 68

CHAPTER 12: PROJECT SCHEDULE MANAGEMENT 70

CHAPTER 13: COST MANAGEMENT 80

EXPANDED VIEW OF COST CONTROL 85
Manage Baseline *85*
Manage Variances *86*
Manage Budget Performance *87*

CHAPTER 14: QUALITY MANAGEMENT 90

WHAT IS QUALITY? 90
OTHER RELATED QUALITY STANDARDS 93
   Why prevention should be emphasized in quality plan 94
METHODS OF QUALITY CONTROL 95

CHAPTER 15: PROJECT RESOURCE MANAGEMENT 100

CHAPTER 16: PROJECT COMMUNICATION MANAGEMENT 109

  COMMUNICATION CHANNEL 113
  COMMUNICATION MODEL 113

CHAPTER 17: PROJECT RISK MANAGEMENT 114

CHAPTER 18: PROCUREMENT MANAGEMENT 125

CHAPTER 19: PROJECT STAKEHOLDER MANAGEMENT 128

CHAPTER 20: PMI® CODE OF ETHICS AND PROFESSIONAL CONDUCT 132

  PMI® CHAPTER 1. VISION AND APPLICABILITY 132
  PMI® CHAPTER 2. RESPONSIBILITY 135
  PMI® CHAPTER 3. RESPECT 137
  PMI® CHAPTER 4. FAIRNESS 138
  PMI® CHAPTER 5. HONESTY 140

APPENDIX A 142

  A.1 HISTORY OF THIS STANDARD 142
  A.2 PROCESS USED TO CREATE THIS STANDARD 143

APPENDIX B 145

  B.1 GLOSSARY 145

This concise book is written for the following purposes:

- Project Management Practice
- Project Management Professionals,
- PMP® Certification exam preparation,
- Last-minute project management exam revision,
- Project Management first timers.

This handy reference book was put together in close collaboration with successful program and project managers, business owners, consultants, entrepreneurs, and students with the objective of presenting concise and accurate information on project management in less than one hundred pages for rapid learning.

AITechConsulting

Dedication

This book is dedicated to my family, friends, and readers that are wishing me the best and success in my next journey of life.

Preface

As a professional engineer, businessperson, consultant, program manager, a practicing project management professional, and most especially a student forever (continuously learning based on projects and operation scenarios), I have put together this book on project management to help those in the pursuit of becoming a project management professional. I attained my certification exam based on work experience and self-learning of the PMBOK® guide. That is, the study of *Project Management Body of Knowledge (PMBOK® Guide)*. This revised book is based on my experience and study of the following books:
   1. Project Management Body of Knowledge – **Sixth Edition.**
   2. PMP® Exam Prep: Rita's Course in a Book for Passing the PMP® Exam.
   3. The PMP® Exam: How to Pass on Your First Try, fourth edition by Andy Crowe.
   4. "Tips on PMP® Exam" by Jim Owens.
   5. Agile Practice Guide.
   6. The Examination Content Guide from PMI®.

Remember, I said self-learning. This is to save cost and maximize the use of my self-initiative and drive. If I can do it, you can also do it.
This book is an expansion of what I learnt and revised weeks before the exam to help me consolidate my knowledge on PMP® topics for passing the exam. The consolidation of knowledge after reading different books, articles, and practicing knowledge gained on program management and system engineering experience enabled me to obtain my PMP® certification. I wish you the best of luck as you read through this book to add to your knowledge and also move you closer to being an expert in project management.

"PMI®," "PMP®," "Project Management Professional," and "PMBOK®" are registered certification marks of the Project Management Institute (PMI®) Inc. in the United States and other nations. This is nonprofit organization helping to drive industry best practices in project management.

Although the author has made every effort to ensure accuracy and completeness of information contained in this book, he can assume no responsibility for errors, inaccuracies, omissions, or inconsistencies contained herein.

Chapter 1: Preparing for PMP® exam

Thinking about taking a PMP® (Project Management Professional) exam? This is a good place to start for information on the purpose of the exam, the makeup of the exam, and where to get more information:

1. The purpose of the exam is to test your general understanding, analysis, and knowledge application of project management.
2. There are two hundred questions in the exam—only one hundred seventy-five of the questions count toward pass/fail score on the exam. One hundred thirty-five of the questions must be passed (68.5 percent). The other twenty-five questions are experimental questions. You will not be able to identify these questions in the exam. Answer as many questions as possible correctly.
3. The exam contains multiple-choice questions. Choose from four answers.
4. Pick the most appropriate answers from the four choices. When there is more than one likely answer, look for the answer that favors the customer.
5. The exams change every time you take it. There are no two PMP® exams that are the same because they are randomly selected from a large database of questions.
6. The time to complete the exam is four hours. It flies quickly if you are well prepared.
7. Practice as many questions as you can from a wide range of selections from books, articles, and the Internet.
8. The Project Management Institute (PMI®) is the not-for-profit membership association coordinating the standards for project management profession. Visit www.PMI.org for more information.

9. There is a fee for taking PMP® exam. Visit www.PMI®.org for details of payment and renewing your certification when you have passed the exam.
10. The Project Management Institute (PMI®) provides a comprehensive handbook, Project-Management-Professional-Handbook for details on the certification application process, requirements, fees, audit process, examination, guiding policies and procedures, and continue certification requirements. You can google the handbook or check on www.pmi.org.
11. Do make sure you read through the latest PMBOK®/PMI® from PMI organization. They have a new version out every couple of year.
12. The PracticePM book is available as a book and as a training audio software CD on www.amazon.com. The software has both audio and text to aid the learning process.
13. The android audio mobile application of PracticePM is also available on Google play store. It is available in English, Spanish, Chinese and several other languages.

Good luck.

Chapter 2: About the PMP® Exam

The PMP exam questions are designed to test the following:
1. Knowledge of project management
2. Application of project management,
3. Analysis of project management.

The table below is a description of the allocation of the PMP® exam. This may change as PMI® revises the PMP® exam, but you can use the table as a general guideline because variation for the values will not be drastically different:

Process Group	Number of Questions	% of Exam
Initiating	26	13%
Planning	48	24%
Executing	62	31%
Monitoring and Controlling	50	25%
Closing	14	7%
Total Number of Scored Questions	175	87.5%
Total Number of Unscored (Pretest) Questions	25	12.5%
Total Number of Questions	200	100%

The professional and social responsibility, ethics, are tested at various level of the process groups.

The key is to know your material. You will be tested on every process group and the knowledge areas of the process group.

You can refer to the examination content outline guide from PMI® for more information.

Chapter 3: On the Day of the Exam

Take the following items with you to the exam center:
1. The PMP® exam eligibility letter.
2. Two pieces of identification (for example, driver's license and passport were acceptable).
3. A nonprogrammable calculator - This was provided on a computer-based exam center.
4. Pencil/Pen - This was provided at the center. But have them with you just in case they run out of it at the center.
5. Snack and water - You can take few minutes breaks between the exams for snack and mind rest.
6. Dress appropriately for the environment and weather.
7. Stay calm, relax, take your time, but you only have four hours.

Other ideas that you should keep in mind to aid in passing PMP® exam:
1. Think PMBOK®/PMI® all the time when answering the questions—not your ways but PMBOK®/PMI®.
2. Memorization is not enough to pass the exam but an understanding of the process group and the functional areas.
3. Use the paper provided for your calculations and to brain dump formulas memorized for the exam.
4. Answer the easy questions first, and then tackle the harder ones afterward. All questions carry equal marks. One point per question. You need to answer at least 160 questions; twenty-five of the questions answered may not count because they are experimental questions, and 135 questions must be answered correctly to pass. Increase your chances of passing by attempting all 200 questions.
5. Look for best the answer. Eliminate the wrong answer first then select the correct answers.
6. Prepare for calculations for Network Analysis and Earned Value.
7. For USA based questions on ethics, Proactive Management Approach the PMBOK® way is the most correct answer.

Chapter 4: Project

The project management team is responsible for determining what practice is good for any given project. There are similarities between projects and operations. This section highlights on what is a *project* and its differences from *operations*.

What is a project?

A project is a temporary endeavor undertaken to create a unique product, service, or result. The result consists of deliverables – unique and verifiable results from the phases of project, such as, documents, product or services.

The following diagram shows a project phased out into iterations. An iteration is a complete project:

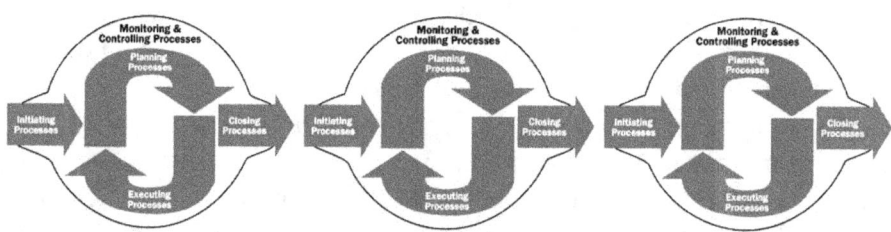

Figure 1: Project Iterations

The following are the characteristics of a project:

- ❖ A project is a temporary endeavor to create a unique product, service, or result.
- ❖ It has a defined purpose and may be in phases.
- ❖ It has definite begin-and-end dates.
- ❖ It has a finite duration. (The duration may be short or long.)

- It may have social, economic, or environmental impacts.
- It creates unique deliverables (products, services, or results).
- A project's complete scope may not be understood at the beginning. The following approach is used to eventually gain full understanding and execution of a project:
  - *Rolling Wave Planning* and *Progressive Elaboration*
    - Developing the project in steps and continuing by increments.
    - A form of iterative waterfall approach with feedback.
    - Projects may change title as it progresses.
- A project must be delivered to the original purpose, changes must be phased, and all assets (resources) must be returned to the corporate pool at the end of the project.
- Project drives change – moving from a current state to another progressive (future) state.
- Project enables the creation of business values that may be tangible (goods or monetary) or intangible (services or benefits).
- Project is initiated in response to demands on organization to remain viable. These demands include:
  - Regulatory, Legal or Social Requirement.
  - Stakeholders Requests or Needs.
  - Implement, change business and technological strategies.
  - Create, improve, fix product, processes and services.

What are the differences between project and operations?

Project	Operations
Project has a finite duration.	Operation is an ongoing and repetitive process.
Project is unique and temporary. It is terminated at the end of its objectives.	Operation is adaptive to new business objectives.
Project is a means of achieving strategic plan.	Operation is a means of continuing the execution of a work plan.

Projects are for strategic achievements

Projects are generally used as a means of achieving an organization strategic plan. The project team may be the employee of an organization or contracted service provider. The common strategic considerations or business drivers for project include the following:

1. Market demands (e.g., the introduction of a new product into the market).
2. Organization or business needs (e.g., the need for business process reengineering to improve daily operations).
3. Technological advancement (e.g., the development of high-speed train for improved traveling time).
4. Customer request (e.g., a customer request to build an estate of apartments).
5. Legal requirements (e.g., the conversion of medical records to electronics document as mandated by federal government [EMR]).

Factors that contribute to successful projects

1. A *Well-Defined Scope*. Project scope must be clearly defined with a purpose.
2. *Sponsor*. The sponsor must have the need, power, and funding.
3. *Budget*. There is money available for the project.
4. *Will to Succeed*. Driven by the sponsor and aided by the project manager.
5. *Approval*. There must be buy in from sponsor and/or senior management.

Portfolio, Programs and Project

- **Portfolio** — A portfolio is made up of a collection of projects, programs, sub-portfolios and operations that are group together for a strategic plan. The strategic plan is aligned with the mission of an organization, body or institution.

- **Programs** – A program consist of sub-programs, projects and operational work group together to achieve the strategic objective of the portfolio.

- **Project** – The full definition of project was described earlier. Projects make up a program and they can also be part of a portfolio.

- The organization of projects, programs and portfolio is based on the following criteria:
    - Organization Strategies
    - Priorities of organization objectives
    - Progressive Elaboration
    - Governance – The guiding principles set by the management to drive the business direction of the organization.
    - Change Requirement
    - Change impact on the organization

Roles of Portfolio, Program and Project Managers

The role of managers or expectations in organizational project management.			
	Projects	**Programs**	**Portfolio**
Scope	Progressively Elaborated over project existence.	Larger scope covering many projects.	Organizational scope derived from strategic objectives.
Change	Implement and managed processes for expected changes.	Manage internal and external changes affecting programs.	Manage all internal and external environment changes affecting the aggregate portfolio.
Planning	Progressively elaborate project into actionable plans through the life of the	Break program into actionable high-level components and create detailed plans	Create guiding processes and communication for the growing portfolio.

	project.	relative to the components.	
Management	Manage the project team per project objectives	Provide program vision and manage project managers and supporting staffs to meet program objectives.	Manage or coordinate staffs supporting the portfolio.
Success	Measure success by project outputs: Products, quality, timeliness, budget compliance and customer satisfaction.	Measure success by satisfaction of needs and benefits fulfilled by program.	Measure success by aggregate investment performance and the resulting benefits realized from the portfolio.
Monitoring	Monitor and control the execution of tasks required to produce the expected result of the project.	Monitor the progress of actionable components defined for the program. Measure progress relative to program goals, schedules, budget and benefits expected from the program.	Monitor changes, resource allocation, performance, results and risk in the portfolio. Measure relative to strategic goals set for the portfolio.

Project Environment

The success of every project also depends on the influences of its environment. The major categories of influences are enterprise environmental factors and organizational process assets.

Enterprise Environmental Factors

This is divided into internal and external environmental factors:

Internal Environmental Factors	External Environmental Factors
Organization Culture, Structure and Governance	Marketplace conditions
Geographic Distribution of facilities and Resources	Social & Culture influences and Issues
Infrastructure	Legal restrictions
Information Technology Software	Commercial databases
Resource Availability	Academic research
Employee Capability	Government or industry standards
	Financial considerations
	Physical environment elements

Organizational Process Assets

This may be grouped into categories, processes, policies, procedures and Organizational knowledge bases:

Processes, Policies & Procedures	Organizational Knowledge Bases
Initiating & Planning	Configuration Management
Executing, Monitoring & Controlling	Financial Data Repositories
Closing	Historical Information
	Issue & Defect Management
	Data collection & Repositories
	Previous Project Files/Documentation for reference.

Chapter 5: What is Project Management?

Project Management — is the application of knowledge, skills, tools, and technique/method to deliver projects on time, on budget, and to specification (or project scope). The project management team is responsible for determining what practice is good for any given project. Whatever practice is chosen for the project, the project managers must be conscious of the triple constraints, and the integrated processes must be applied accordingly.

Triple Constraints — a project quality is defined by the triple constraints:
1. Project scope,
2. Time, and
3. Cost

Integrated Process Group — The process groups must be applied across the project:
- Initiating
- Planning
- Execution
- Monitor and Controlling
- Closing

Management by Projects — A number of organizations are adopting management by projects, structuring some of their operations into projects, but not all their operations.

Knowledge and skills required for project management

The practice of project management requires the understanding and the use of the following subject areas:

Project Management Body of Knowledge (PMBOK®)—This is a book that is published by the Project Management Institute (PMI®). It presents a set of standardized terminologies and guidelines that are generally accepted as project management information and practices. Visit *www.PMI®.org* on how to obtain a copy for your study and project management practice. The PMBOK® is organized into three sections:
1. The project management framework:
    a. Organization or project environment
        i. Social, economic, and cultural environment
        ii. Physical environment
        iii. Intellectual and political environment
    b. Project life cycle
2. The standard for project management practice. These are the five project management process groups:
    a. Initiating
    b. Planning
    c. Execution
    d. Monitor and control
    e. Closing
3. The project management knowledge areas:
    a. Scope
    b. Schedule
    c. Cost
    d. Quality
    e. Resource
    f. Communication
    g. Risk
    h. Procurement
    i. Stakeholders
    j. Integration of the above areas.

Standard - This is a documented process established by consensus and approved by a regulated body for repeated use and guidelines.

Regulation - This is a government-imposed requirement. It is a mandatory compliance. A project may have to be executed under the guidance or restriction of government regulations. Project managers are expected to understand the project environment and comply with the regulations.

General Management Knowledge and Skills - These are general knowledge and skills required for project management:
- Financial management
- Purchasing and procurement
- Sales and marketing
- Strategic planning
- Health and safety
- Contract and law
- Manufacturing and distribution
- Logistics and supply chain
- Information technology

Portfolio Management - This is the management of collection of projects, programs, sub-portfolios and operations for strategic objectives. The components of a portfolio may be related or may not be related or inter-related. The following are some of the characteristics of a portfolio:
- Not interdependent.
- Managed based on specific goals.
- Efficient use of resources.
- Managed by senior management.

Program Management – This is the management of a collection of related projects, subprograms and activities for efficient use of available resources. It is the application of knowledge, skills, tools, and technique to a collection projects, subprograms and activities to meet program requirements while optimizing the use of available resources across the program.

A Program Management Office (PMO) is setup to manage program or programs. This is where the management and distribution of resources for the program takes place.

The PMO helps to identify strategic key methods, standards, and tools for program and project managers to follow in managing and delivering key strategic initiatives (i.e., projects) while sharing information and documentation. The PMO may serve any of the following roles in program management:

- **Supportive** – A consultative role with very low control – Provision of templates, best practices, training, project repository on past projects and lesson learned.

- **Controlling** – Provision of support and compliance requirement on the program(s). Moderately ensuring, with the right people skills, that all or most supportive tools provided and are utilized as expected on the program.

- **Directive** – This is a hands-on management of the projects, subprograms and activities in the program. High degree of control.

Subproject — Large projects may be divided into manageable components to facilitate project management processes. The manageable components are sub-projects.

Business Value, Project Management, Operations Management and Organization Strategy

Project Management	Operations Management	Organizational Strategy
Helps to achieve organizational goals when coupled with organization strategies.	Oversees, direct and controls business operations.	Created by organization to address objectives derived from present situation and desired strategic changes.
Focused on dedicated	Management of	A continuous

project with definite end time to address strategic changes. For example; creation of a new product or service.	ongoing business process to support strategic changes.	evaluation of present and future business situation to produce new strategic changes.
Driven by corporate strategies	Driven by corporate strategies and end result of project.	Driven by corporate governance – Strategic directions and key performance indicators.
Focus is on bridging the gap between business value and organization strategy with effective and result oriented project management.	Focus is on effective management of day-to-day operations to support maintenance and improvement of business value.	Focus is on obtaining great business value for all investments made by the corporation.

Who is a Project Manager?

A project manager is the person responsible for performing the following roles on a project:

- Satisfy the needs of the project, task, team and individual needs on the project.
- Lead the team responsible for completing the objectives of a project.
- Works closely with program and portfolio manager to achieve project objectives.
- Collaborates with business analyst, quality assurance manager and subject matter experts to complete project objectives.
- Leverage project management knowledge across the project
- Apply project management knowledge to accomplish the tasks on the project.
- Utilizes personal, interpersonal, ethical, and conceptual skills to effectively manage a project to success. What are your interpersonal skills?

- Leadership
- Team Building
- Communication
- Motivation
- Political and Cultural Awareness
- Negotiation
- Coaching
- Proactive Communication
- Influencing
- Decision Making
- Conflict Management

- Project Managers are expected to work on all these skills mentioned above to make them very effective on projects.
- The best project managers have demonstrated superior relationship and communication skills while displaying a positive attitude at all levels of the organization structure.
- Keep abreast with the current industry trends. Technology, project management practice, standards, processes, market niche, supporting tools and economic forces are moving targets.
- Participates in continuous education, training and development Contributes to educating other project managers through available resources. One of my contributions is this book.
- Finally, here is what I do to keep my PMI Talent Triangle® up to date:
    - Technical Project Management
        - Involvement PMI/PMP education
        - Use of Agile or project management tools.
        - Hands-on technical implementation for effective knowledge to manage related project.
        - Managing technical projects.
    - Leadership
        - Continuous participation in Toastmaster for effective communication.
        - Systems Development Management at work.
        - Leadership role at social clubs.

- Interpersonal relationship – Dealing with people. Extremely essential. Practice and practice to perfect this area.
- Setting and managing expectations.
  - Strategic and Business Management
    - Participation in organization strategic goals that lead to various portfolio, programs and projects for the business.
    - Attending all-hands meeting to understand cooperate strategic directions:
      - Mission
      - Goal & Objectives
      - Product & Services
      - Operations
      - Market
      - Competition
      - Priorities.
      - Business Risks & Issues
      - Financial Implications
      - Business Value
      - Cost Analysis
      - Scope, budget, schedule and quality

Chapter 6: What is Project Life Cycle?

In organizations, every project and the management of project are in context of the processes, tools, and techniques appropriate and applicable to the organizations. Project life cycle is a representation of the phases that connect the projects from the beginning to the end. The following diagram shows the relationship between project life cycle and project process group. Study the diagram and phase a project to gain an understanding of how it applies to your organization:

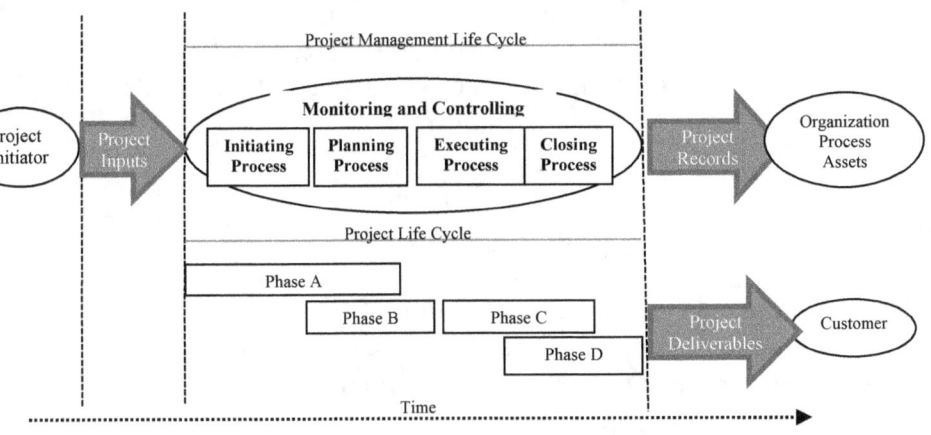

Figure 2: Project Management Lifecycle.

The phases A, B, C and D are collections of activities to be done for the project deliverables. Phase A may have one of more activities in it, likewise, the other phases shown on the diagram.

The following are some of the terms associated with project life cycle:

- **Project Management (PM)** - PM provides the oversight to ensure that the project is managed within the framework applicable to the industry and it is delivered on time, on budget, and to specification.

- **Project Processes** - The project processes are the steps to be undertaken by the project team in each phase of the project. The steps are usually clearly defined in the methodology of the lifecycle. The following are some of the steps that are common in the engineering field that may be applicable in other industries:
    - *System Implementation*
        - Analysis
        - Design
        - Development
        - Implementation
    - *Rational Unified Process (RUP)*
        - Inception
        - Elaboration
        - Construction
        - Transition
    - *Agile Software Development Approach*
        - Small iterations of product development:
            - Analysis
            - Design
            - Development
            - Implementation

- **Project Delivery** - This is the execution of tasks defined for the steps in the project phases. These tasks are undertaken by the project team to fulfill the project requirement.

- **Deliverables** - The deliverables are artifacts or outputs of tasks defined in the project delivery.

- **Schedule Compression**
    - **Fast Tracking** - This is the reordering in the sequence of activities of a project. The phases off the project are re-arranged so that the next phase begins before the deliverable of the current phase. Some of the activities are performed in parallel instead of in series.
    - **Crashing** — this is the adding of more resources to project

activity so that it can be completed quickly.

- **Project Phases** – Projects are generally divided into phases to ease the management process, planning and control. The phases are logical grouping of the tasks, work or processes required to accomplish the objectives of the project. The suggested guiding principle for dividing your project into phases is to ensure that each phase produces a milestone at the end of its completion. Phase your project based on the methodology provided within your organization and be creative base on professional management standard. The following are the **types of relationships** that can be applied to the phasing process of your project:

    - **Sequential** — the execution of a phase within a project must complete before the next phase starts. The project is generally more predictable more this may lengthy the project schedule.

    - **Overlapping** – The execution of a phase starts before the completion of the previous phase. This may help to crash the project to meet tight deadline. Resources may be required to multi-task or multiple resources working in parallel.

- **Phase Gate or Phase Review** – This is held at the end of a phase to review the deliverables, project performance and progress. The reference documents for the phase review includes but not limited to the business case, project charter, project management plan, benefit plan and go or no-go decision based on out of phase gate or review. In systems engineering, which is my area of expertise, we have operation readiness, site acceptance criteria, test results review. Apply the relevant phase gate documents for your business or industry.

As a project manager, evaluate the complexity and constraints of the project, apply either or combinations of the type of relationship to the phasing of the project for ultimate successful delivery within time and budget.

Types of Project Life Cycle

Figure 2.1: Project Lifecycles.

❖ **Predictive, Linear or Fully Plan-Driven** — This type of life cycle is applied to projects that have clearly defined path which may be based on standard industry practice, or product development projects with clearly defined processes. The processes may be sequential or overlapping, but the end result is predicable based on the set of steps to be executed for the project.

The style of project management applicable to this type of life cycle may be regarded as **Traditional Project Management**, because the goals and solution are known to the stakeholders.

- ❖ **Iterative and Incremental** - The iterative and incremental lifecycles apply to projects where a number of predictive lifecycle must be applied to produce a result that adds to overall project result. The predictive lifecycle here is called iteration. The iteration is repeated several times to produce many results that are added together for the final outcome of the project. The final outcome of the project is said to be incrementally produced from many iterations. For example, the making of cars, each part is produced from their own iterative (repetitive) manufacturing process, incrementally assembled to make the car.

  They style of project management that may be applied to this lifecycle is **Agile Project Management** – clearly defined goals, final solution is incrementally produced from prioritized list of solutions that are iteratively defined from customer interactions.

- ❖ **Adaptive Life Cycles** – This method is highly suitable for dynamic business environment where there is changing needs from customers and/or project sponsor(s). New requirements are formulated to address changes, prioritized, and listed on a backlog. Small iterative projects are executed to address the list in the backlogs. The customers and project sponsors are involved on a daily basis to compile the backlog list.

  They **Agile Project Management** style is generally applied to this lifecycle because of the uncertainty in project requirements. The goal of the project is driven by business changes; dynamic task priorities, solutions are defined on the fly to meet project goals.

- ❖ **Extreme Cycles** – This method is highly suitable for research and development environment where project goals and solutions are not known, very high risk and high change type of project environment. There is heavy involvement of customers and project sponsors to define the goals and solutions of the project.

The **Extreme Project Management (xPM)** style may be applied because neither the goal nor solution is clearly defined for the project.

The **Emertxe Project Management (MPx)** style may also be applied to this extreme lifecycle where the solution is well defined but the goal is not defined for the project.

What is the project process (or life cycle) in your organization?

As mentioned earlier, this may be industry specific depending on the product or services to be produced from the project. But irrespective of what your answer may be to this question, a project process or project life cycle must have the following attributes:

- Pre-Project Work
- A start of the project
- Organization and Preparation
- Execution of work
- Completing or closure of the project.

You can generically apply these attributes to small and large projects in your personal life. To ensure that all projects, personal or corporate are delivered on time within budget. The following cost level must be taken into consideration when planning with the project life cycle:

❖ **Pre-Project Work**
  o What is the need or business driver?
    - Feasibility Study
    - Compile a business case and for the project.
    - What is the benefit before investing time, money and resources.
    - Get buy-in from management.

❖ **A start of the project**
  o Develop the project launch and authority document – the **Project Charter**.

- The final output of the project can easily be influenced at this stage.
  - The risk and uncertainty of project are much higher at this point.
  - The detailed requirements are still being defined and refined for acceptance by stakeholders.
  - The cost of material and head count is low at this point.
  - The cost of change to project scope is low at this point.

- ❖ **Organization and Preparation**
  - Develop the project guide – the **project management plan**.
    - This describes processes to be followed in executing, monitoring and controlling the project.
    - The processes described are industry, needs and organization specific for the success of the project.
    - The mission, vision, execution and complete integration of the project areas detailed in project management plan.
  - The cost of material and head count are low at this point.
  - The cost of change to project scope and produce is low but increasing at this point.
  - Gradual increase in cost as project scope becomes clearer and more resources are identified for the project.

- ❖ **Execution of work**
  - The project management plan is put to work by the project manager.
  - The full execution of project is on the way, project cost is increasing or stabilized, and risk level decreases as requirements have been clearly defined for the customer or with customer.
  - The project sponsors have agreed with the direction of the project, decreasing risk and uncertainty.
  - But the cost of changing the direction of the project or make changes to the output is now higher.

- ❖ **Closure of the project**
  - Execute the project closure guidelines defined in the project management plan.
    - Validation of Delivery
    - Acceptance criteria

- Transfer of deliverables
    - Documentation of operations
    - Documentation of project completion
    - Finalizing the project closure
- Little or no risk of uncertainty
- Cost of changes to project output is definitely higher at this point.
- Lesson learned is documented for reference on similar and future projects.

Chapter 7: Project Stakeholders and Organization

Who are the project stakeholders?

Project stakeholders are individuals and organizations that are actively involved in the project or whose interest may be affected as a result of the project execution or completion. The following are some of the stakeholders on a given project:
- Individuals, Organizations, and Customers
- Project Team
- Sponsor - Provider of financial and political support
- Influencer—Influences project managers' decisions for desirable outcomes
- Benefits positively from the project—Positive stakeholders (e.g., oil refinery)
- Negative stakeholders—See negative outcomes from the project (e.g., location of oil refinery)
- Sellers of products or services to the project. Vendors, Contractors or supplier for the project.
- Program Management Office (PMO) - Coordinators of project management standards, assets, and templates.
- Partners – Business partners or joint ventures in support of the project.

The following graph shows the power of stakeholders on a project over its life relatively to the cost of changing the project base on their request.

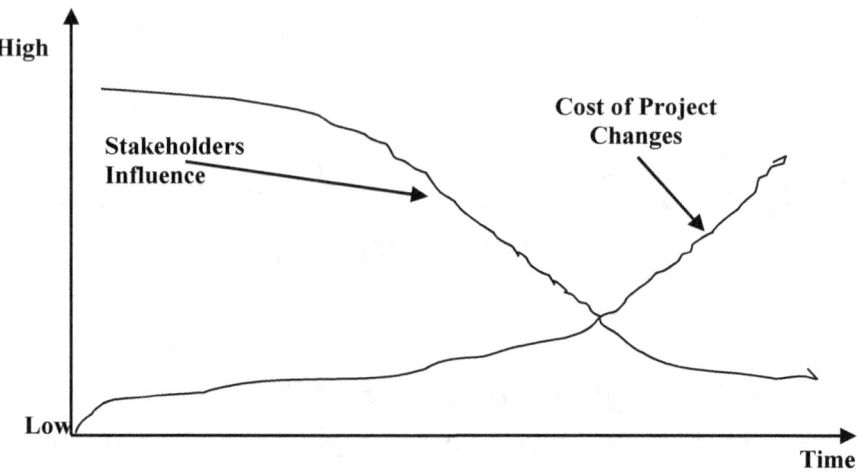

Figure 3: Stakeholders' Influence and Cost of Change.

Organizational Structure and Project Organization

It is important for project managers to understand the organizational structure and framework in which they are going to manage projects. The following questions must be answered for the project to be undertaken by a project manager:

What is the organizational structure for this project?

Is the organization project focused? To fully understand and answer the organizational structure for a project, the project manager should investigate the response to the following questions:

- ❖ **Framework**
    - o What is the project organization?
    - o Who do you report to?
    - o Is matrix organization?
    - o What is the power and authority of the project manager?
    - o Is this a project-driven organization?
    - o Is this a hierarchical organization?
    - o Who is the project sponsor?
    - o Who does the sponsor report to?

- ❖ **Structure**
    - o How does a project get delivered?
    - o How does a project get initiated or accepted?
- ❖ **Culture**
    - o What is the organization's culture?
    - o Do they value people?
    - o Must everything be done at all cost?

What is the organizational framework?

Most projects are executed within an organization with a framework in place that guides the overall operation of the organization. It is very important that the project manager understands the organizational framework to manage a project effectively within an organization. The following questions should help to investigate the organizational framework:

- ➢ **Structural-Organization Chart**
    - o Who reports to whom?
    - o Who has the power to ensure that the project gets delivered successfully?
- ➢ **Human Resources**
    - o How are employees treated?
    - o Do the employees come first or project comes first?
    - o What is the work ethics? Is forty hours per week or overtime expected?
    - o Are the organization people driven?
    - o What is the attitude to training?
    - o Is there on-the-job training?
    - o Is the project the most important?
- ➢ **Political Framework**
    - o **Internal Politics**—who must be happy to ensure that your project is successful?
    - o Who has the power?
    - o **External Politics**—who do you have to work with externally to ensure the project is successful?
    - o Who is your ally?
- ➢ **Symbolic**
    - o What is the dress code?
    - o Is the boss approachable

- Is this a hierarchy organization?
  - Is this a formal or friendly environment?
  - What is the norm?

Organizational Structure

The type of organizational structure surrounding a project often determines how resources are managed and their availability for projects. Power and authority will be determined by the organizational structure. The organizational structure also helps to answer most of the questions posed in previous sections. The following are the types of organizational structure applicable in various organizations:

Functional Organization

- This is a traditional business organization where you have the head, the CEO (Chief Executive Officer), broken down into the appropriate business/functional areas with the respective VP, managers, and functional area owners.

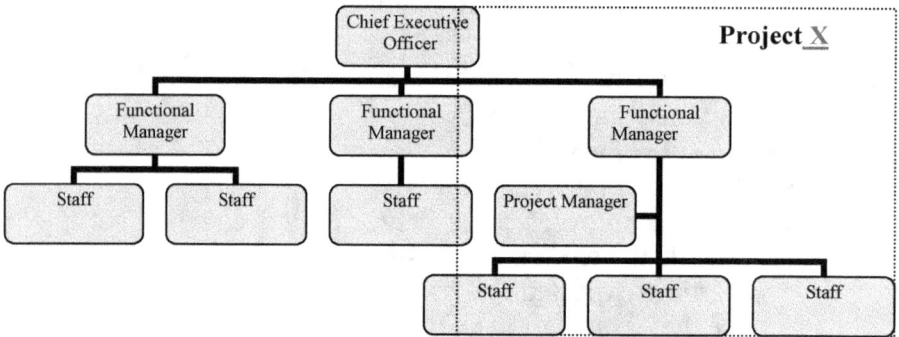

Figure 4: Functional Organization.

- Project is delivered within the business units.
- Project managers are also line managers who have other responsibilities other than the projects.
- Team members are from the same business units as indicated by the box labeled Project X.

Projectized Organization
The characteristics of a projectized organization include the following:
- ❖ Organization is focused mainly on projects, no other responsibilities.
- ❖ Project-based organization—The organization is project based and has a head with project managers leading the project areas and reporting to the head. The team members report to the project managers.
- ❖ The project managers have high to almost total authority.

Figure 5: Projectized Organization.

- ❖ The resources available are dedicated to the project.
- ❖ The project manager controls the budget.
- ❖ This type of organization is common to consulting companies that mainly focus on project delivery. This project organization does not exist in traditional organizations.

Matrix Organization
- ❖ This is the most common form of organization, a combination of the traditional functional business organization and the project organization.
- ❖ Cross-functional business areas determined by engagements or projects.
- ❖ There are three types:
- **Weak Matrix**—Project for a business unit is executed by team members from multiple business units as indicated by the shaded area.
  Advantage: Special skills and knowledge can be pulled from various business units of the organization for the success of the project.
  Disadvantage: The team members still have to report to their line managers. There may be conflicts between objectives of the project

39

manager and the line managers of the various team members. The project manager assumes a coordinator role, minimal authority, and control on resources.

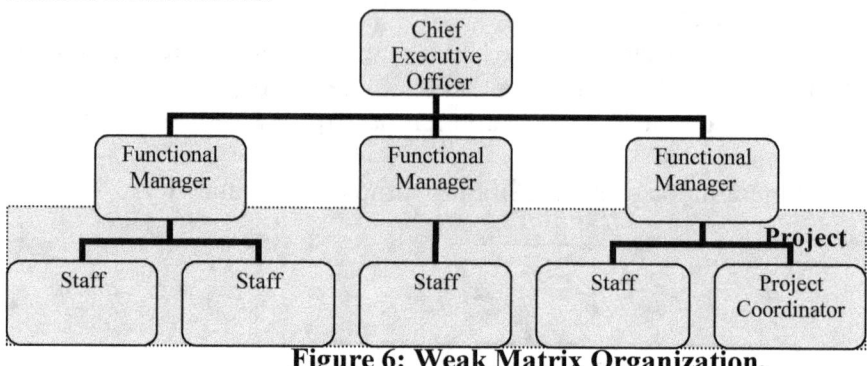

Figure 6: Weak Matrix Organization.

- **Balanced Matrix**—Similar to weak matrix organization with the exception of providing a dedicated project manager with considerable authority and full-time administrative staffs.
- **Strong Matrix**—Strong project-oriented organization characteristics but with limitations imposed by functional organization.

  Advantage: 1. Special skills and knowledge can be pulled from various business units of the organization for the success of the project. 2. Dedicated project managers and administrative staffs.
  Disadvantage: 1. The team members still have to report to their line managers. 2. There may be conflicts between objectives of the project manager and the line managers of the various team members.

Figure 7: Strong Matrix Organization.

Composite Organization

- ❖ This type of organization combines all the various types of organizational structures.
- ❖ A department may have its dedicated project team.

Figure 8: Composite Organization.

Comparison of the Organizational Structure by Project Manager Skills

Functional Organization
1. Limited project management skills.
2. Part-time project management availability.
3. Wide range of authority. High degree of authority over team members.
4. Functional manager has the budget ownership.
5. Staff availability is part-time.
6. Wide range of staff skills.

Projectized Organization
1. High project management skills.
2. Full-time project management availability.
3. Full responsibility and authority.
4. Project management has budget responsibility.
5. Full-time staff availability.
6. Highly dedicated staff skills.

Weak Matrix Organization
1. Limited project management skills.
2. Part-time project management availability.
3. Low authority over team members.
4. Functional manager has the budget ownership.
5. Staff availability is part-time.
6. Wide range of staff skills.

Strong Matrix Organization
1. High project management skills.
2. Full-time project management availability.
3. Medium authority over team members.
4. Project manager has the budget ownership.
5. Staff availability is part-time and full-time.
6. Wide range of staff skills.

What is the organizational culture?

Organization culture is an important environment factor that also contributes to the success of a project. Project managers should make attempts to answer the following questions in determining the culture that surrounds their projects. The answers to these questions will help them to make effective decisions that will aid the success of their projects:

1. What is the corporate identity of the organization? Leader, follower, or innovative?
2. What is the corporate versus individual emphasis? Do we focus more on profit (bottom line) or if the employees are happy? A profit or employee-driven organization or well balanced?
3. Business integration: Share or compete for budgets? Some organizations expect their business units to compete for the research and development money to push the overall success of the company.
4. Does the organization take risk? Risk tolerance? Does the organization believe that risky project will bring more success?
5. What is the organization focus? Long or short term? To be profitable in five years or in one year?

6. What is the overall company overall maturity? Startup, mature, or established company? This determines how project managers should operate the projects (project/product/company maturity). Is project management methodology well embraced in the organization? What is the project management methodology and project life cycle?

These factors determine how successful your project will be in the organization because they are the environments that support the project.

Other Supporting Systems and Office for Project Organization

Program Management Office (PMO)
The PMO serves the following functions to aid project success:
- Management of multiple projects enabling project template sharing.
- Provides advisory support on projects.
- Recommends policies and procedures where necessary.
- Provides administrative support to project managers.
- Serves a centralized management point for project managers.

Project Management System
The project management systems are the tools, techniques, methods, and procedures for managing projects.

Project Governance
The project governance is the guiding framework put in place by organization to ensure project decisions are made in alignment with stakeholder needs, expectations and strategic objectives of the organization. The role of project governance is to govern capital investment and maximize the value from project investments.

Chapter 8: What is Project Management Process?

The *project management process* by PMI® standards consist of processes recognized as good practice globally, and across industry groups, to enhance the chances of success over a wide range of project executions. The PM process ensures that we have the management in place *to support* the project process, and we have the management structure in place *to do* the project process. The processes help to ensure effective flow of the project throughout its life cycle.

The *project manager and team*, in collaboration, are always responsible for determining what processes are appropriate for any given project. The project management processes as defined in the PMBOK® guide is a combination of the five process groups and the nine knowledge areas.

Other processes that may apply in project management depending on your industry include:

- **Product-Oriented Process** – Clearly defined steps to be followed in creating the product of the project.
- Customer-Centric Process – Processes defined by the project organization in creating a product or services tailored to their customers.
- **Plan-Do-Check-Act Cycle** - The project management process group is based on this principle.

The *project management process groups* per PMI® standards are

44

as follows:

- **Initiating** - Define and authorize the project phases. Is this a valid project? Should this project take place?

- **Planning** - Define and refine project objectives and scope to be achieved. We define the steps required for the schedule, project process, resources, budget planning. This defines how the project is done.

- **Executing** - Project delivery. The process integrates resources and people to carry out project objectives. This is the actual completion of work required to deliver the project— members of the team execute the tasks of the project. The most hours and expenses are incurred during this phase.

- **Monitoring and Control** - This is an active process through the project life cycle executed by the project manager. He or She regularly measures and monitors progress so that corrective actions can be taken when meaningful. The process ensures that we are on time and on budget and delivering to expectations.

- **Closing** - This is about gaining the final acceptance of the project. It brings the project to an orderly end.

Project Management Process versus Project Process

		Project Life Cycle		Rational Unified Process (RUP)	What is your project life cycle?
Monitor & Control	Initiating				
	Planning				What are the phases in your project lifecycle?
	Executing	Analysis		Inception	
		Design		Elaboration	
		Development		Construction	
		Implementation		Transition	
	Closing				

Figure 9: Project Life Cycle.

The execution of project life cycle takes place during the execution process of project management process groups. The project life cycle is determined by the project manager and team members of the project. They determine what project life cycle and the rigor of implementation in the execution phase. Every industry has its applicable project life cycle. What project life cycle is applicable to your organization?

Project Management: Level of Activity Chart (Time versus Effort)

The following chart is the level of activity over time in the project management process groups:

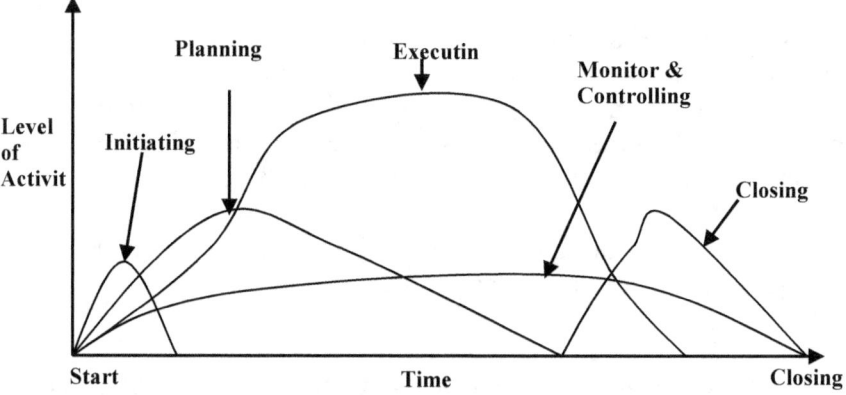

Figure 10: Level Of Activity Chart.

The following points should be noted for the level of activity chart and PM process groups:

Initiating - An intense and short activity at the beginning of the project.

Planning - Ramps up early at the beginning project and then levels of over the course of the project. The ramp is due to resource planning, project planning, and scope planning; all the initial planning takes place here. The continuation of planning on the chart is due to ongoing planning and re-planning required for keeping the project on track.

- **Executing** - Project execution starts slowly and ramps up over the life of the project. It falls toward the end of the project and has the most activities, that is, the delivery of the project (analysis, design development, and implementation).

- **Monitoring and Controlling** - As shown on the graph, this goes through the entire life of a project. It ensures that the project is on time, on budget, and according to specification.

- **Closing** - It brings the project to orderly close. Closing is generally brief and a fast process to bring the project into closure.

The process groups are executed once per project or once per phase of a project. They can be done at each phase of the project life cycle. The process groups are repeatable steps for each phase of the project life cycle. The phases of the project life cycle are dependent on the organizational industry standard, but for this purpose, we used analysis, design, development, and implementation.

Why iterate project management process groups?

Figure 10.1: Level Of Activity Chart.

Project iterations are necessary for large projects to breakdown projects into manageable processes. Traditional planning of engineering projects is organized around product or service breakdown and development. This approach was inherited from manufacturing and construction industries. Today and the future are about process breakdown into manageable and repeatable processes. Each manageable process produces different deliverable that ultimately results to the overall objective of the project. This approach of process breakdown at project management process groups and project life cycle (e.g., IBM, In the *Rational Unified Process [RUP]*) enables the following benefits:

1. To revalidate project for risk assessment and continuity of the project.
2. Re-planning as needed based on evaluation or revalidation.
3. Introduce improvement where necessary.

Summary of Project Management Process

Provide SOW, Contract, Business case & other project supporting documents.

Project Sponsor

Initiating: Identify Stakeholders, Create Project Charter, & Initiate Procurement Process.

Project Sponsor & Project Management

Planning: Create Project Management Plan, Document Requirement, Create Procurement list, Make or Buy Decision, Create Resource Schedule, Initiate Monitoring & Controlling Process.

Customers & Project Management Team

Executing: Execute Project Management Plan, Request for Proposal, Award Contract, Approve changes per control measurements, review and execute control measurements, Create deliverables, Provide Training.

Customers & Project Management Team

Closing: Provide final products or services to customers, Review & accept deliverables per control measurements.

Customers & Project Management Team

Monitor & Controlling: Review change request, provide project status, set quality control measurements, execute quality control, generate performance reports, review deliverables and provide supporting documentation.

Customers & Project Management Team

Chapter 9: Planning a Project from End to End Using PMBOK®

The table in the next page describes the process groups relative to the knowledge areas per project management processes:

Knowledge Areas	Process Group				
	Initiating	Planning	Executing	Monitor & Controlling	Closing
Project Integration Management	• Develop Project Charter	• Develop Project Management Plan	• Direct and Manage Project Execution • Manage Project Knowledge	• Monitor & Control Project Work • Perform Integrated Change Control	• Close Project or Phase
Project Scope Management		• Plan Scope Management • Collect Requirements • Define Scope • Create WBS		• Validate Scope • Control Scope	
Project Schedule Management		• Plan Schedule Management • Define Activities • Sequence Activities • Estimate Activity Durations • Develop Schedule		• Control Schedule	
Project Cost Management		• Plan Cost Management • Estimate Costs • Determine Budget		• Control Costs	
Project Quality Management		• Plan Quality Management	• Perform Quality Assurance	• Perform Quality Control	
Project Resource Management		• Plan Resource Management • Estimate Activity Resources	• Acquire Project Team • Develop Project Team • Manage Project Team	• Control Resources	
Project Communications Management		• Plan Communication Management	• Manage Communication	• Control Communication	

Knowledge Areas	Process Group				
	Initiating	Planning	Executing	Monitor & Controlling	Closing
Project Risk Management		• Plan Risk Management • Identify Risks • Perform Qualitative Risk Analysis • Perform Quantitative Risk Analysis • Plan Risk Responses	• Implement Risk Responses	• Monitor Risks	
Procurement Management		• Plan Procurement Management	• Conduct Procurement	• Control Procurement	
Stakeholder Management	• Identify Stakeholders	• Plan Stakeholder Management	• Manage Stakeholder Engagement	• Control Stakeholder Engagement	

Here are the steps to be followed with reference to the PMBOK® table:

Initiating

Develop project charter. The project charter is needed to define the scope of the project and also gain the formal approval for the official start of a project.

Identify Stakeholders. The overall success of a project depends on the people or organization involve in the project. These are the stakeholders. They provide the requirements, execute the tasks involve, operate the results and control the outcome of the project.

Planning

Develop project management plan. This is a critical component of the project management process. A well-developed project management plan helps to guide the successful execution of the project.

Plan Scope Management. This task manages how scope is collected, defined, validated and controlled to ensure that only the required work will be completed for project success.

Collect requirements. Using the project charter, the project manager and project team facilitate workshops and interviews, brainstorming exercise, and group activities to define the detailed scope for the project.

Define scope. All collected requirements and the overall project scope is agreed with the stakeholders.

Create WBS. Develop work breakdown structure. Deliverables are broken down into manageable smaller tasks required to achieve the scope.

Plan Schedule Management. This management process is for ensuring that policies, procedures and documentation are in place for planning, developing, managing, executing, and controlling the project schedule.

Define activities. This is a list of activities identified during the *Create WBS*—the list of activities to be executed to produce the deliverables defined for the scope of the project.

Sequence activities. In what order should the activities listed be executed? A project life cycle approach might help to achieve this process.

Estimate activity duration. Estimate the time required to execute the activities defined in previous process.

Develop schedule. Using all the activity information defined in previous steps, develop a schedule using available tool, for example, Microsoft Project software.

Plan Cost Management. This process formulates the policies, procedures, and documentation for planning, managing, expending and controlling cost on project.

Estimate cost. Using time and the resources as parameters, determine the overall cost of the project.

Determine budget. Develop budget for estimated cost of resources, materials, services, and contracts needed for the project. The determined budget should include contingency plan in case of cost overrun.

Plan Quality management. This process establishes the quality standard required for the project and ensures that the project management process incorporates the standard. The application process of the standard is also documented for the project. The "do it right the first time" principle and total quality management approach.

Plan Human Resources Management. This process provides structure the development of a plan for human resources; Providing guidance on when resources are needed, and when they exit the project based on schedule, training process, team communication process, conflict resolutions, and effective teamwork.

Estimate activity resources. Estimate the resources needed to carry out the activities defined for this project. Resources may include materials, human resources, building, hardware, and software. Basically, the resources needed to accomplish the execution of a successful project.

Plan Communications Management. This process is the planning of how information will be shared or communicated on a project and what information will be communicated and distributed on the project. The planning is driven by stakeholder's requirements and organizational needs.

Plan Risk Management. This is the process of creating a proactive risk management plan. The plan should include identified risks, risk analysis, and planned risk responses.

Identify risks. Create a list of possible risks on the project.

Perform qualitative risk analysis. Using expert judgment, experience, and probability, weigh identified risks; assign a level of prioritization; and rank them.

Perform quantitative risk analysis. Using expert judgment, experience, and probability, weigh identified risks by assigning a projected monetary value to each risk and rank them.

Plan risk response. Using expert judgment, experiences, and results from risk analysis, prepare proactive responses to the risks identified. These responses are guides for managing the risks.

Plan Procurement Management. This is the planning of what to buy, how much to buy, where to buy, when to buy needed (materials, services, and contracts) resources for the project.

Plan Stakeholder Management. This process is for planning the identification of project stakeholders, defining approach of stakeholder's engagement, managing communication with stakeholders, and monitoring the relationships and strategies with stakeholders.

Executing

Direct and manage project execution. This is the process where the project manager and project team perform actions to execute the project management plan. The project management team directs the performance of the project activities and manages the interfaces of the project organization.

Perform quality assurance. This is the continuous improvement process for the project. Improve and correct deficiencies as part of the project life cycle, analyze and audit process, recommend corrective actions, improve standards and processes. The update the project management planned accordingly.

Develop project team. Build the project team by collocation (war room), training, team building exercise, recognition and reward, setting ground rules, and team performance assessment.

Manage project team. Manage the project team by observing performance, monitoring issues, resolving conflicts, and completing performance appraisals.

Distribute information. Using the defined list in the communication management plan, distribute project information to the respective stakeholders using the predefined models and methods.

Implement Risk Resources. This is the process of implementing agreed-upon risk response plans.

Conduct procurement. This is the execution of the activities defined in the procurement management plan. These activities include short listing qualified vendors or sellers, evaluating seller proposals, conducting bidder conferences, selecting sellers, and awarding procurement contract.

Manage Stakeholder Engagement. Stakeholders' engagement on the project must be continuously managed, while meeting their expectations and addressing issues via effective communication of any changes on the project.

Monitoring and Controlling

Monitor and control project work. This process is performed to measure the project deliverables and the process by which they are produced against the planned processes and standards defined in the project management plan.

Perform integrated change control. All the needed or requested changes in the project must be assessed for impact analysis on the project. This is the control process that enables the project team to evaluate the acceptability of a change for execution.

Verify scope. Scope verification is ensuring that the deliverables from the project meet the documented scope. Gold plating is not allowed and neither should the project team under deliver to the project scope. The formal acceptance of stakeholders on project deliverables takes place during this process.

Control scope. Controlling the scope of the project is ensuring that change requests are within project scope. Any change request outside the project scope is channeled through the Perform integrated change control process.

Control schedule. This is part of the perform-integrated change control to monitor schedule changes and the factors influencing the changes.

Control cost. Monitor cost changes, factors contributing to the changes, preventing cost overrun, monitor cost performance and variances from baseline.

Perform quality control. This is the monitoring of products and deliverables on a project to determine their conformance to relevant quality standards.

Control Resources. This is ensuring that the allocated and assigned physical resources are available as planned. This also involves monitoring planned versus actual utilization of resources and taking corrective action throughout the project to maintain the plan.

Control Communication. This is ensuring that communication needs for stakeholders and the related project are to expectations.

Monitor risks. This is the tracking of risk identified in the project, identifying new risks, and executing the corresponding risk response plan defined in the project management plan.

Control Procurement. This process involves managing contracts between the seller of services or materials to the project and project management team. All deliverables and work performed are reviewed against the content of the contract. If any change to the contract, the appropriate contract change control system is applied.

Control Stakeholder Engagement. This is the process of monitoring stakeholder involvement in the project and making adjustments in strategies to ensure that the end result meets stakeholder's expectations while achieving success in the project.

Closing

Close project or phase. This is the process of closing the project or phase of the project in an organized manner. Lesson learned is captured, contract closure is collaborated with the respective vendors, and all organization assets are updated with project documentation, forming part of historical information.

Close procurements. This is the formal closure of the contracts with the vendors or suppliers. All deliverables and product(s) are verified for acceptance, and contracts are terminated as needed, ideally, amicably.

Now that we have defined our approach for all the activities of the process groups for the end-to-end planning of the project, we need to expand on each process and integrate them together for the success of a project. The following sections describe the knowledge areas and expand on the approach for each process in the process group.

Chapter 10: Integration Management

The project integration management knowledge area enables the project manager to have a high-level view of the project from start to finish. This is the **starting point** of a project engagement. You identify, define, combine, unify, and coordinate all relevant processes within the project management standard that are applicable to the project at hand. The following processes are the guiding principle from PMI® standard:

- ❖ Develop project charter.
- ❖ Develop project management plan.
- ❖ Direct and manage project execution.
- ❖ Manage Project Knowledge
- ❖ Monitor and control project work.
- ❖ Perform integrated change control.
- ❖ Close project or phase.

The following sections describe the listed project management processes and highlight the work to be carried in each process.

Develop Project Charter

The project charter is first deliverable from initiation phase, which officially indicates the start of a project. It is a high-level one—or two-page document that broadly describes the project.

The project charter covers the following:

- ❖ **Introduction into the project** - Description of the problems as described in the Statement of Work (SOW) issued for the project.

❖ **Business Objective** - This is the main component and must be developed with the business sponsor(s). Business cases to be considered for this factor includes the following:

Market demand	Business needs
Customer request	Technological advancement
Legal requirement	Ecological requirement
Social need	

❖ **Preliminary Cost/Benefit** - What are the benefits for this project? These benefits are needed to sell the project to the senior management and sponsor. What is the payback period on this project? To determine the cost and benefits, consider the following project selection method:

- **Benefit Measurement Method**—Monetary benefit and cost.
- **Constraint Optimization** - Mathematical/calculus calculation.
- **Benefit Cost Ratio (BCR)** - If greater than 1 (one), good benefit over the cost. Project product sold more for the cost of the project (BCR = Selling price/cost price).
- **Economic Value Add (EVA)** - The value created by project for its stakeholders. Keep the money in the bank if the return on project will be of a lesser value.
- **Internal Rate of Return (IRR)** - Project return as interest. The bigger the return, the better the project.
- **Net Present Value** - How much is the product of the project worth right now with the cost of the project taken out of the worth value? The bigger the better.
- **Present Value** - How much is the product of the project worth right now? The bigger the better.
- **Opportunity Cost** - What is the cost of the other opportunities we missed by investing our money in this project? Do not miss big opportunities. We can miss out on the smaller opportunity.

- **Payback Period** - The quicker it takes to recover the investment on a project, the better. A shorter payback period is better than a longer one.
- **Return on Investment (ROI)** - What percentage of return is made by investing on a project? Bigger is better.
- **Return on Investment (ROIC)** - This is a measurement of how much is the return on every dollar spent on a project. Bigger is better.

❖ **Agreement or Contracts** – The high-level obligations of the contracts, letter of understanding or service level agreement established with the customer must be highlighted in the project charter. This is setting the standard and direction of the project.

❖ **On completion** of the project charter, a formal approval must be documented confirming the acceptance of the project to officially take place. The business sponsor, project manager, and senior management should all be in agreement on the content of the project charter and its feasibility. This expert judgment and facilitation of the review sessions will also be applicable in closing out this process of developing the project charter.

Develop Project Management Plan

On receiving the approval of the project charter, the work required to complete the project must be planned. The project management plan document must be developed because it outlines briefly or in detail how the project is managed, executed, and controlled. This is more like a project guide.

Per PMI®, the project management plan is expected to contain the description on the following headings:

❖ **Scope Management Plan** - The management and control of project scope.
❖ **Schedule Management Plan** - The management of project schedule.

- **Cost Management Plan** - The management of project cost, money allocation, and sourcing of funding.
- **Quality Management Plan** - The management of planning, assurance, and control on the project.
- **Process Improvement Plan** - The management of continuous improvement from the "plan, do, check, act" cycle or quality wheel feedback implementation on the project.
- **Human Resource Plan** - The administration and behavior management of project resources.
- **Communication Management Plan** - The management of planning, formation, and distribution of information on the project.
- **Risk Management Plan** - The management of planning, identification, analysis, monitor, and control of risk.
- **Procurement Management Plan** - The management of purchases of products and services needed from vendors to perform project work.
- **Schedule Baseline** - The original plan plus all approved changes. Approval by customer, sponsor, and the project manager.
- **Cost Performance Baseline** - The original plan cost plus all approved changes. Approval by customer, sponsor, and the project manager.
- **Scope Baseline** - The original scope plus all approved changes. Approval by customer, sponsor, and the project manager.
- **Change Management Plan** - The management of change process on the project.
- **Configuration Management Plan** - The management of identification, changes, storage, and status reporting on project deliverables.
- **Requirement Management Plan** - The management of activities required to gather, handles changes, decide, and document requirements.

The listed headings do not have to be in a single document; they can be separated into their own documents depending on the scale of the project and how detailed the plan is required. Other headings that you may considered is at the discretion of the project manager, such as the management of change, configuration and requirements,

Direct and Manage Project Execution

In direct and manage project execution, the project manager spends most of the time managing resources, cost, and time. The team members are executing the work packages and creating deliverables. The project manager integrates the team and work using the project management plan to create the project deliverables, change request, corrective and preventive actions. The project management plan is the master plan.

Manage Project Knowledge

This is to facilitate continuous improvement in project execution by using existing knowledge and creating new knowledge to achieve project objectives. The existing knowledge are derived from lessons learned, documents and deliverables from previous phases of projects. Your organization may use tools like confluence, sharepoint, or eroom to facilitate the management of project knowledge. The project manager ensures that project knowledge continues to grow and applies the knowledge to assigned projects. The PMO office is generally responsible for managing project knowledge across the organization.

Monitor and Control Project Work

The project manager continuously measures the project execution and deliverables against expectations as defined in the project management plan. He/she makes decisions based on results to ensure that the project is going according to plan. Specific areas of measurement by the project manager include project schedule, project information and distribution, issues and risks, resource performance, project performance, and procurement process.

Perform Integrated Change Control

Project managers are expected to have a structured method of managing change in project because change is inevitable in every project. The Perform Integrated Change Control process ensures that all changes requested or needed on the project are evaluated for their impact on the project. An impact analysis on the various sections of the project management plan is carried out to ensure success of the project. The output of this process includes: approved change request and requested change request.

All change requests feed directly into direct and manage project execution process.

Close Project or Phase

This process guides the project manager in shutting down a project in an orderly manner. The key tasks for this process include the following:

- ❖ Create documentation and archive.
- ❖ Capture lesson learned and keep history for future projects.
- ❖ Close contract.
- ❖ Update organization assets (including historical project portfolio).
- ❖ Recover organization assets.
- ❖ Put a final closure base on expert judgment review.

Chapter 11: Project Scope Management

This is the management of defining all the work required to complete the project. Inclusive in this knowledge area is ensuring that only the work required for the project is executed to expectations. The project scope must be clearly and well defined and communicated to the stakeholders. The following are the activities to be managed under scope management:

- ❖ **Plan Scope Management**
  - Define your scope definition, deliverables, changes and review processes.
  - Review the project charter, organization culture, available resources, and infrastructure, to construct a plan for managing the scope from end-to-end.
  - Review scope management plan with all relevant stakeholders.

- ❖ **Collect Requirements**
  - Facilitate requirement-gathering interviews, workshops or activities.
  - Apply proven methods to collect requirements:
    - Interviews with relevant stakeholders
    - Discussion with focus groups:
      - Subject Matter Experts
      - Customers or End-Users
      - Stakeholders
    - Brown bags or Requirement workshops
    - Group Creativity Activities
      - Brainstorming sessions

- Idea-mind mapping
- Idea grouping or Affinity diagram
- Decision Analysis Tree using different and relevant criteria – Multicriteria decision analysis.
- Questionnaires and Survey technique
- Observation
- Prototyping
- Benchmarking – Comparison current state with desired future state based on best practices.
- Context or use case diagram.
  - Refine and document requirements.
  - Manage the requirement collection activities per defined project scope in the project charter.
  - Create requirement traceability matrix to facilitate requirement management.

❖ **Define Scope**
  - Determine the final product or service by defining the detailed project scope based on the following:
    - Project charter input.
    - Collected Requirements.
    - Policies, procedure and templates.
    - Decisions from key workshops, meetings or survey.
    - Historical information from similar projects.
    - The detailed scope should include:
      - Clear definition of the product or service to be developed.
      - Agreed level of quality for acceptance.
      - List of deliverables expected from the project.
      - Accepted requirements and phased out requirements. Project results may be released in phases. Define expected results per phases to set expectations.
      - Constraints and Assumptions made for scope definition.

- **Create Work Breakdown Structure (WBS)**
  - A top-down decomposition of project deliverables to create the work and subdivided into manageable smaller components for project management.
  - Create WBS per planning, scope, requirements, your industry or organization-imposed standards, available resources and assets.
  - Use hierarchical block diagram from representation of decomposition.

- **Validate Scope**
  - Work with the stakeholders to ensure they approve the scope of the project.
  - Use traceability matrix to track the development of all requirements.
  - Ensure and plan a formal acceptance of each deliverable to obtain sign off.
  - Establish a timeline for the review and feedback. Client needs to have a specified timeline to come back with feedback.
  - Turn around. Insist on a single set of comments. A formal acceptor must provide the feedback or comments to avoid conflicting comments.
  - Interim acceptance process must be established.
  - Put an acceptance process in place by section of the deliverable document.
  - For example, Section 1 is accepted and no further changes are required.
  - Section 2 is still open for changes. There are minor changes to be added before acceptance.
  - Resubmit.

- **Control Scope**
  - The defined scope is the reference point for all scope creep or changes. Refer to the scope management plan or establish a process to manage the project scope changes. (Change management.)
  - The change management plan should have clearly defined

process for managing scope and requirement changes.
- Control changes to deliverables of scope, such as requirement documents using established configuti0on management process and tools.
- Integrate change:
  o Schedule team
  o Risk
- Establish a formal acceptance process for project scope and requirement changes.

Expected Outputs

The expected output from scope management knowledge area when executed per PMI® standard includes the following:

- ❖ **Scope Management Plan** – Documentation of how project scope will be defined, verified and changes will be controlled.
- ❖ **Project scope statement**
  o Work breakdown structure (WBS) with work package identifier, control account, work packages, unique account identification, cost summation, schedule summation, and resource information.
  o WBS Dictionary with work package identifier, work package description, account codes, cost estimation, control account, milestone list, list of resources, statement of work, and responsible organization.
  o Scope Baseline = Scope Statement + WBS + WBS Dictionary. This is an important output that feeds into the following processes:
  o Control Scope
  o Define activities.
  o Estimate costs.
  o Determine budget.
  o Plan quality.
  o Identify risks.
  o Plan procurement.

- ❖ **Requirement Documentations**
    - o Business Requirements.
    - o Stakeholder Requirements.
    - o Functional or Solution Requirements.
    - o Project Requirements – SLA, compliance etc.
    - o Assumptions, dependencies and Constraints.
    - o Transition Deployment Requirements.

- ❖ **Traceability Matrix** – Requirements mapping for ease of traceability during and after implementation.

- ❖ **Requested Changes**—these are not necessarily approved changes.

Chapter 12: Project Schedule Management

The project schedule management is a knowledge area that covers the definition of activities, resource estimating, and the development of scheduled processes to be managed by the project manager. The primary input for executing the processes defined for time management is the scope baseline. The scope baseline is inclusive of scope statement, work breakdown structure, and the work breakdown dictionary. The processes for project time management and what they entail are as follows:

- ❖ **Plan Schedule Management**
    - o This process provides the overall guidance for managing the project schedule over the life of a project.
    - o The input to this process includes the:
        - Project Management Plan – Scope baseline
        - Project Charter – Summary of milestones and approved project requirement summary.
        - Organization Culture.
        - Available Human Resources & Skillsets.
        - Available Tools and Assets:
            - Historical information on previous projects
            - Procedures
            - Templates
    - o The overall guidance is achieved by:
        - Defining policies, procedure and templates for end-to-end development of project schedule:
            - Planning
            - Development
            - Managing
            - Executing
            - Controlling

- The specific that may be defined under this heading include:
  - The project scheduling tool and methods.
  - Activity duration and contingencies for estimation.
  - Unit of measurement for resources, days, hours, weeks.
  - The WBS templates or framework for consistency.
  - Coordination and maintenance style for the project schedule.
  - Earned value management
  - Reporting formats
  - Documented process for the schedule management.

❖ **Define Activities**
  - Document the work to be performed.
  - Define activities base on work and schedule, *not* on deliverables.
  - Further decompose the work defined in the Work Breakdown Structure (WBS) into activities.
  - Decompose one Work Breakdown Structure (WBS) to one resource.
    - Apply *Rolling Wave Planning*. Develop detailed activities and assign corresponding time frame. It provides a certain degree of time estimation accurate enough to plan the project or next phase. The following table is an example of rolling wave planning:

Activity	Deliverable	Work/Schedule
Analysis	DLV 1	Time 1 (20 days)
Design	DLV 2 DLV 3	Time 2 (30 days) Time 3 (40 days)

Activity	Deliverable	Work/Schedule
Development	DLV 4	Time 4 (40 days)

| Project Management | DLV 5 | Time 5 (150 days) |

- ❖ **Sequence Activities**
  - Use any of the three types of dependencies to clarify activity sequence
    - Mandatory dependencies – Legal, contractual or inherited sequence of activities.
    - Discretionary dependencies – Preferred logical sequence of activities.
    - External dependencies – Dependencies on non-project related activities. The PM has no control on these activities.
    - Internal dependencies – Project related activity dependencies.
  - Define the sequencing between the tasks.
  - Define the type of dependencies:
    - Finish to Start
    - Finish to Finish
    - Start to Start
    - Start to Finish
  - Focus on the mandatory dependencies; this may include optional dependencies but may bring in more complexities.
  - Include lead (head start) and/or lag (delay) time.
  - Draw dependency diagrams:
    - **Activity on Node (AON)** or **Precedence diagram** (the most common style for depicting activity dependencies). Suggested by Project Management Institute (PMI®) group. Here are the characteristics of this diagram:

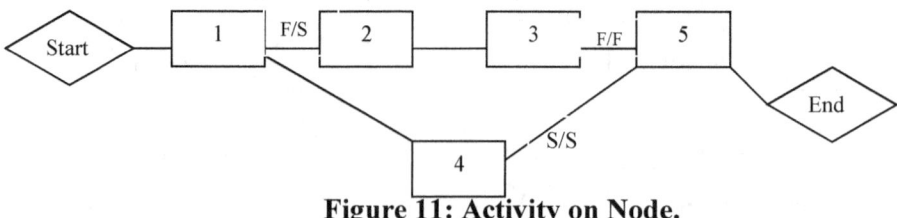

Figure 11: Activity on Node.

- Task 1 has tasks 2 and 4 as its successors
- Task 2 has task 3 as its successor
- Task 5 has tasks 4 and 3 as its predecessor.
- Start/start relationship between 4 and 5.
- Finish/finish relationship between 3 and 5.
- F/S between relationship between 1 and 2.
- Tasks are put on the node/box.

- **Activity on Arrow (AOA)** - This type of dependency diagram is rarely used on projects. The activities are represented by the arrows connecting the nodes. The nodes are typically circles as shown in the following diagram:

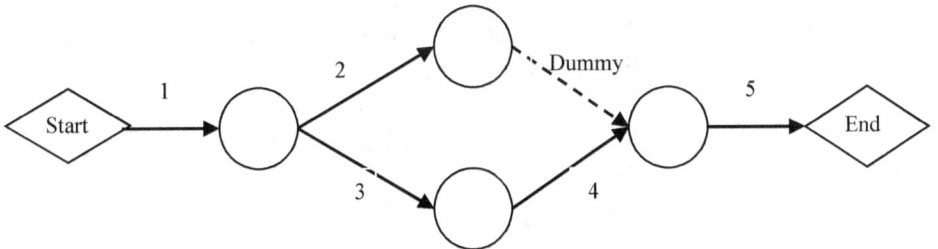

Figure 12: Activity on Arrow.

Here are the characteristics of this diagram:

- The activities are on the arrows.
- There is no information in the nodes, but they are there to allow us to create dependencies.
- Tasks 2 and 3 are dependent on 1.
- Task 4 is dependent on 3.
- A dummy node is created to allow task 2 to depend on the end of the project and task 5.
- The dotted arrow indicates a dummy activity.
- It only represents finish/start style relationship.

❖ **Estimate Activity Durations**
  o The estimation of activity duration is needed to

develop an accurate schedule. The input for estimating duration includes the following:

- **Resource Calendar**
  - The following factors must be considered when scheduling resource availability. For example:
    - Forty hours does not equal forty hours,
    - Full-time resource for forty-hour work week,
    - Sick time
    - Read e-mail,
    - Vacation time, and
    - Attending department meetings.
- Estimated Activity Resources
- Project Scope Baseline
- Organization Process Assets or and Project Historical Information.

  - Methods for estimating duration accurately include:
    - Guess/Roll dice,
    - Monte Carlo analysis – Quantitative analysis method to determine the period required to execute work.
    - Analogous – Estimation using historical data from similar project.
    - Parametric– Algorithmic method for calculating cost or duration using historical data and project.
    - *B*ottom-up estimating,
    - Multiple estimators (compare savings), and
    - PERT (Program Evaluation Review Technique). Developing multiple estimates for each task:
      - Pessimistic (P), Optimistic (O), and a Most Likely (ML)
      - (P + 4ML + O) divide by 6 = Estimate

- In general, the following factor must be considered when estimating duration:
    - Amount of work.
    - Team.
    - Actual effort, not duration.
    - Forty hours work.
    - One resource = one week.
    - Focused on the amount of work required to complete the job, not the duration.
    - Software applications may be used to calculate the duration leaving time to focus on work required to complete the tasks.

❖ **Develop Schedule**
  - Refer to your schedule management plan on defined method for developing the schedule.
  - Using software preferably, although this may be done manually, develop the project schedule using the following inputs:
    - Activity list, attributes and estimated durations
    - Work Breakdown Structure (WBS)
    - Network diagrams showing dependencies among tasks.
    - All available information on resources such as Requirements, Calendar etc.
    - Your industry standard, templates and available assets for schedule development.
  - Develop the schedule using any of the following thought process:
    - Determine early start (ES), late start (LS), early finish (EF) and late finish (LF) for each activity using any of the following analytic methods:
      - Critical path method – What is minimum project duration?
      - Critical chain method – How much buffer is required in the project schedule for resources and uncertainties?
      - Resource Optimization –
        - Resource leveling based on available resources – Are critical resources available full-time or needs to be shared with other projects? Develop schedule based on availability of resources.

- - o Resource Smoothing – Are resources availability limited? Develop schedule within the limit of available resources.
    - o What-if Analysis – Prepare for unexpected situations on the project. What if there is a delay in resource delivery or availability? Model the situation.
    - o Simulation – Monte Carlo Analysis – using three-point estimates to determine various possible activity durations for the project.
    - o Lead and Lags – Apply leads and lags time to compensate for delays and head starts.
    - o Fast Tracking and Crashing can be used to compress the project schedule.
  - Iterate through the process to develop the final schedule.
  - Produce the following charts to represent the project schedule:
    - Bar Charts
    - Milestone Charts
    - Network diagrams
    - Document assumptions and constraints
    - Resource Histogram
    - Contingency Reserved schedules.

❖ **Control Schedule**
  - o The majority of effort occurs here to ensure project is completed in a timely manner.
  - o Monitor project progress and manage changes in schedule baseline.
  - o Minimize risk by quick recognition of deviation from plan and taking corrective and preventive actions.
  - o This process involves having a number of methods in place to track progress, integrate changes, and manage against project schedule baseline. The specific methods and details are as follows:

- **Critical Path Method**

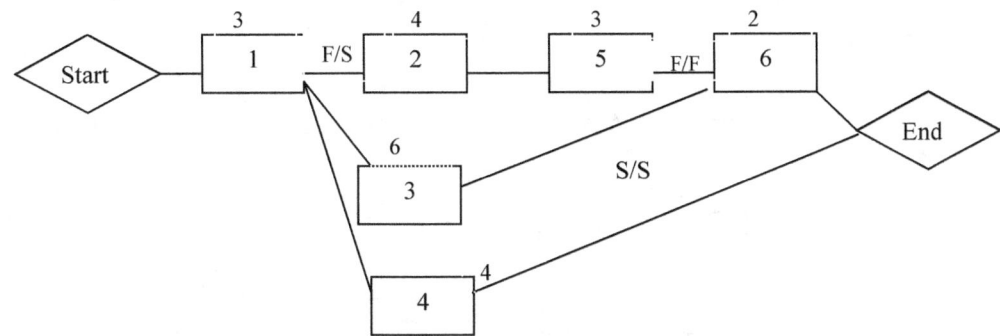

Figure 13: Critical Path Method.

- The critical path in the plan that has the longest duration to the end of the project. This effectively determines the end date of the project.
- The critical path in the above diagram is route tasks 1, 2, 5, and 6 (duration: 3, 4, 3, 3) = 12.
- Control and monitor the tasks on the critical path to make sure nothing impacts them because they affect the end date of the project.
- Monitor tasks that are near the critical path that may become critical path due to small changes.
- This is the most effective method for monitoring the end date of a project.
- A project management tool may be used to calculate for near critical path, that is, the slack or float. The bigger the slack (or float), the further away from critical path.

- **Resource Leveling**
    - This is the development of a project schedule based on limited resources. A resource-limited schedule is developed:
        - To ensure an optimal team size for the project
        - To ensure full utilization of resources.
    - A coco model may be used to determine the optimal team size.

The following resource level chart that shows the utilization distribution on a project:

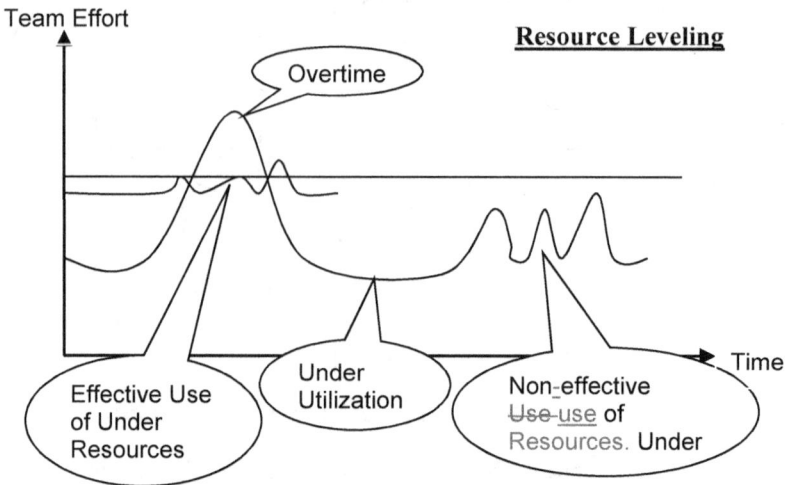

Figure 14: Resource Leveling Chart.

- **Track Progress**
    - Team must provide weekly status report, inclusive of report time needed and remaining to complete a task.
    - Work with team members to get information on tracking project schedule.
    - This could be a tasking process, but work with the team to track progress.
- **Integrate Changes**
    - Integrate changes into the project schedule.
    - The project software will recalculate the project plan. It is necessary to work with team members to ensure project timeline is not drastically affected in the project.
    - Implement effective change management process. Update project plan based on approved changes.
    - Manage against baseline. Measure changes against baseline and manage accordingly.
- **Schedule Compression**
    - There are two commonly used methods for schedule compression.
- **Fast Tracking**
    - What can be done to make the project progress faster?
    - Review dependencies and eliminate where possible. Make the tasks run in parallel where possible.
    - Introduce lag where possible and start some tasks earlier.

- Cost may not be increased, but project risk is slightly increased since original dependencies as discretionary are ignored, and parallel execution of tasks has now been introduced.
- **Crashing**
  - Change project environment to improve end date.
  - Introduce new resources and optimal number of resources.
  - Introduce new project management tools to facilitate the process.
  - Cost is certainly increased. Too many resources do not necessarily improve project schedule linearly.
  - Examine critical path tasks for schedule compression since they have the highest impact on the project end date.

Chapter 13: Cost Management

Project cost management is for managing the processes to ensure that projects are completed within the approved budget. These processes include the estimating, budgeting, and controlling costs. The following sections describe the processes of project cost management:

- ❖ **Plan Cost Management**
    - o Put a structure on how the costing of project resources will be managed:
        - Define processes, policies and procedures for cost management.
        - Make templates for documentation to facilitate adherence to defined processes.
        - Ensure all processes of cost management are covered in process definition:
            - Planning – Refer to the scope, schedule baselines and any other information to ease cost planning.
            - Managing – Process and procedures may be in place for financial control at corporate level. These should be followed with approved project specific approach.
            - Expending – Review and/or define procedures and policies for project spending.
            - Controlling – Set cost baselines and define how variance will be measured against baseline.
- ❖ **Estimate Cost**
    - o Create detailed estimate for each and every element in the work breakdown structure. The total project cost estimate must include the following:
        - Cost to deliver each work breakdown

- structure element.
  - Cost of human resources.
  - Cost of materials.
  - Cost of Supplies.
  - Project life cycle costing (trade-off analysis). Spend more now on planning and design and spend less later on implementation, verification, and maintenance.
  - Cost of quality.
  - Cost of overheads.
- The cost to be estimated may be classified into the following:
  - **Direct Costs**—Direct salary cost of team, direct cost for purchasing material.
  - **Indirect Costs**—Fringe benefits, insurance, telephone charges, supporting cost for the projects. Storage, transportation, hotel bills, etc.
  - **Fixed Costs**—Cost a unit for a resource, material, and equipment.
  - **Variable Costs**—For every unit, hour, supply, or time, there is a cost associated with the usage.
  - **Sunk Cost**—Unrecoverable cost that have been expended upon a project.
- **Cost Variance**
  - The change of cost over time must be considered when estimating cost. For example, inflation and depreciation of materials (e.g., vehicles, computers).
  - The change of cost over volume. Supplier's agreement (one to ten quantity cost more than eleven to one hundred in quantity).
- **Estimating Technique**
  - Techniques for estimating cost for order of magnitude, conceptual, preliminary, definitive to control estimates include the following:
    - Group Decision Making Technique
    - Reserve Analysis
    - Analogous Estimation - Expert judgment based on history and previous

experience.
- Parametric Estimation - Parametric unit cost times the number of required units.
- Unit Cost Based on Effort - Cost of resources.
- Vendor Bids/Fixed Price Analysis - What is the cost of project per vendor?
- Bottom-Up Estimating - The most accurate method. The cost estimation at work packages or activities level.
- Three-Point Estimates - PERT (Program Evaluation Review Technique):
  - Most Likely (tM)
  - Optimistic (t0)
  - Pessimistic (tP)
  - Triangular Distribution (tE) = (t0 + tM + tP)/3
  - Beta Distribution (tE) = (t0 + 4tM + tP) / 6
- **Estimation Type**
  - The following are some of the type of estimation that could be used for cost estimation and also applicable to time estimation:
    - Rough Order of Magnitude [-50% to +100%]
    - Conceptual Estimate [-30% to +50%]
    - Preliminary Estimate [-20% to 30%]
    - Budget Estimate [-5% to +10%]
    - Definitive Estimate [-15% to +20%]
    - Control Estimate [-10% to 15%]
  - Accuracy of estimates will increase as the project progresses through the project lifecycle.

❖ **Determine Budget**
  - This is the summation of individual cost estimates to determine the total project cost or cost performance baseline. This process also involves dealing with cash management and forecasting. The cost budget should include the following:
    - Aggregated Costs—The cost aggregation of direct, indirect, fixed, and variable costs.
    - Developed cash flow that is based on the

estimates—A month-per-month cash flow for cash management.
- Cost Baseline— Approved changes in estimated total project cost.
- Contingency (unknown cost variance). The need to have reserve for contingency.

o A practical approach to determining cost budget (using a bottom approach on the work breakdown structure) is cost aggregation:
- Work Package Cost = Cost of Activities
- Control Account = Sum of Work Package Costs
- Project Cost = Sum of Control Accounts in the Project
- Cost Performance Baseline = Contingency Reserve + Project Cost
- Cost Budget = Management Reserve + Cost Performance Baseline

o The accuracy of the determined budget for effective cost management and control is aided by applying the following in the summation process:
  i. Round the budget to the next appropriate level (to the thousandths, hundredths, etc.).
  ii. Define project budget with degree of precision +/- 50%.
  iii. Define project budget with degree of confidence.

o Project Budget Accounting—every organization has a defined approach for defining their budget within an accounting principle. The project manager is expected to work with their account department on how budgeting is done. The following accountings principles that are common to most organizations may be used to qualify project viability (or selection) for budgeting and implementation:
- **Present Value (PV)** - Apply an expectation of future interest rate to determine the current value of money to be spent on a project (or **future value**, apply future interest rate to determine the return on

the money to be spent). It might be better to keep the money in the bank for better return at the end of the term. Higher present value is desirable.
- **Net Present Value (NPV)** - This is the same as the present value but with the cost of project factored into the calculation.
- **Rate of Return (ROR)** - The expected rate of return, inflation, and interest rate.
- **Payback Period** - What is the length of return? Shorter payback period is preferred.
- **Return on Investment (ROI)** - The bigger, the better is the project for investment.
- **Return on Investment Capital (ROIC)** - The higher, the better. Net income divided by capital invested.
- **Internal Rate of Return (IRR)** - If the project was an interest rate, what would you prefer? Bigger is better.
- **Benefit Cost Ratio (BCR)** - Greater than one is good.
- **Economic Value Add (EVA)** - After tax profit.
- **Opportunity Cost** - The smaller the opportunity cost of choosing a project, the better the project. This is really the cost of the other opportunities missed.

❖ **Control Costs**
  o This is a proactive process to ensure that spending on a project is monitored and controlled. It ensures that costs in a project are within the planned budget and any change in costs is easily detected.
    o The proactive approach for controlling costs include the following:
      - *Manage cost baseline per month*. The goal of this process is to deliver on budget and to the plan cash flow. It ensures that the project expenditure is in line with the plan, and project needs are in line with the planned cash flow.
      - *Manage variances*. Measure the variances,

manage and adjust the cost baseline if necessary. Adjustment to the cost baseline will need the approval of senior management and project sponsor.
- *Manage budget performance.* Monitor how project is progressing—on time, on budget; on time, below budget, etc.

Expanded View of Cost Control

Cost management is about cost estimating and ensuring that project is delivered within budget with measures and control in place. The following is an expanded view of the measures for monitoring the cost of a project:

Manage Baseline
1. Review and approve charges on the project.
2. Manage changes.
    a. *Approved changes.* Manage changes through the change control process to ensure integrated change control of project baseline.
    b. *Estimate variances.* Manage time spent on project activities to minimize variances on cost. The pluses and minuses of the variances should be managed and communicated to the appropriate management. Make adjustment where necessary to keep project within budget.
    c. *Price variances.* Monitor price estimates and actual prices of materials and resources. Manage all price variances to ensure all variances are within the project budget.
    d. You may reduce scope based on approved changes to adjust baseline cost.
3. Monitor the coding of charges.
4. Charges are mapped to the appropriate project code.
5. Monitor invoices and the mapping of project codes.

6. Monitor vendor payment and all charges applied to the project.

Manage Variances

1. Variances in project management plan are inevitable. Gather the facts that are causing variances on the project and address those facts.
2. *Variance analysis.* Do the root-cause analysis to see what can be done to improve the variances.
3. *Trend analysis.* Measure the trends of changes in amount versus time. Plot the actual cost against cost baseline for detailed analysis of trends on the project. The following graph is a representation of managing variances with trend analysis.

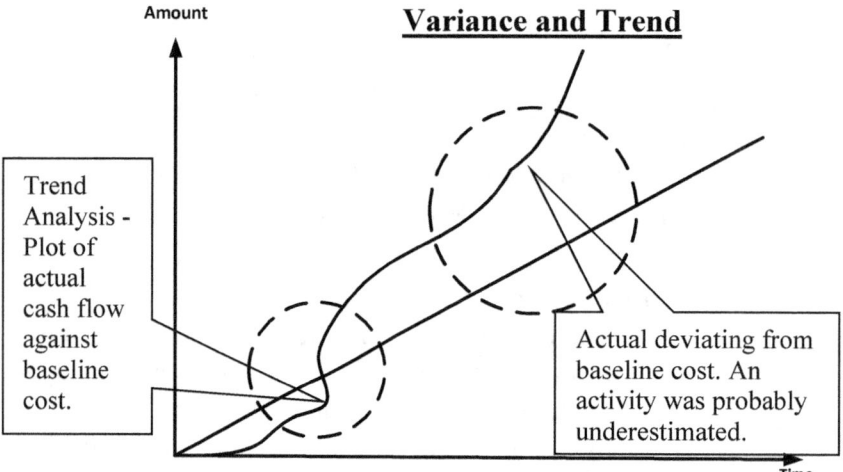

Figure 15: Manage Variance Chart.

Manage Budget Performance

The management of budget performance is done using various performance measurement techniques including the following:

- ❖ **Earned value analysis** - The measuring of actual project performance against original plan. The earned value technique involves mapping budget to schedule and developing the key values for the measurement of scheduled activity, work packages, or control accounts. The following formulas define the key performance indicators when earned value analysis is being used to manage budget performance:
    - o Planned Value (PV) = The percentage of work that should have been completed at a point in time × Budget at Completion (BAC).
    - o Earned Value (EV) = Percentage of work actually completed × Budget at Completion (BAC).
    - o Actual Cost (AC) - This is the actual cost of the project.
    - o Cost Variance (CV) = Earned Value (EV) - Actual Cost (AC).
    - o Schedule Variance (SV) = Earned Value (EV) - Planned Value (PV).
    - o Cost Performance Index (CPI) = Earned Value (EV) / Actual Cost (AC).
    - o Schedule Performance Index (SPI) = Earned Value (EV) / Planned Value (PV).
    - o The following graph illustrate the relationship of these KPIs, relative to time and cumulative cost:

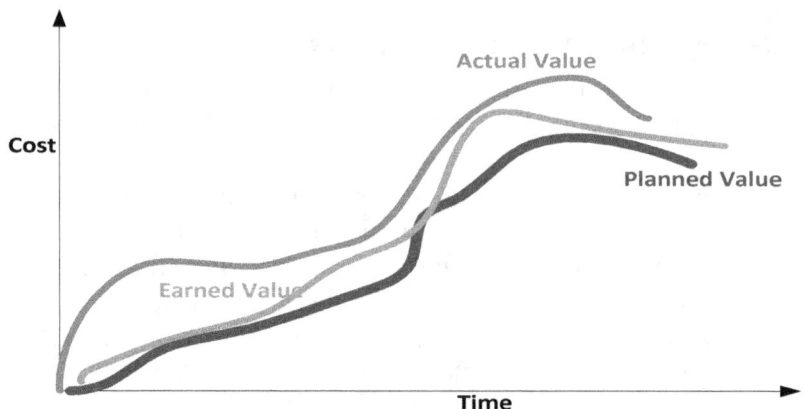

Figure 15.1: Earned Value Analysis.

- ❖ **Forecasting** – This is the estimation of project cost based on project work performance and any supporting information that could impact the project. The key performance indicators (KPIs) that could help to assess the cost or amount of work to complete the scheduled activities include the following:
  - Estimate at Completion (EAC) = Budget at Completion (BAC) / Cost Performance Completion.
  - Estimate to Completion (ETC) = Estimate at Completion (EAC) — Actual Cost (AC).
  - Variance at Completion (VAC) = Budget at Completion (BAC) — Estimate at Completion (EAC).
  - To-Complete Performance Index (TCPIc) - This is the cost performance that is required to be achieved with the remaining resources to meet set management goals. The ratio of cost to finish outstanding work to the remaining budget. The equations TCPI include:
    - TCPI = Work Remaining / Remaining Funds.
    - TCPI = (BAC - EV) / (BAC - AC).
    - TCPI = (BAC - EV) / (EAC - AC).

- ❖ **Project Performance Review** - A schedule-based performance review to measure budget and deliverable of milestones. The indicators of performance review include the following:

- On Time-On Budget - The project is on time and to budget.

- Ahead-Over-budget - The project is ahead of time and over-budget.

- Ahead-Under-budget - The project is ahead of time and under budget.

- Behind-Over-budget - The project is behind schedule and it is over-budget. This is a bad state of project.

- Behind-Under-budget - The project is behind schedule and it is under budget. Adjustment must be made to the schedule or budget for project to continue successfully.

Chapter 14: Quality Management

What is Quality?

Quality is delivering product that is in conformance to requirements, delivering product or services that is fit to use, satisfying the customer (no gold plating— not delivering more than what is promised because quality will be compromised), building prevention into the project quality plan rather than inspection, continuous process improvement, and building quality process and standards into the project planning

The following project quality management processes determine the policies, objectives, and responsibilities expected from a project to meet the requirements from the customer or sponsor. Project quality management consists of the following:

- ❖ **Plan Quality Management** - This is to identify the quality expectations or requirements to be built into the project, and to ensure that the quality process is well defined and communicated in the project. The following steps are followed during the planning of quality management:
    - o Define Quality Management Plan
        - Build quality into the project planning. The project quality management plan should include team inspections, walkthrough, and review. Build the time into the project schedule.
        - Define quality metrics and standards based on the type of project, industry and customer requirement.
        - Define quality checklist.
        - Build in customer quality expectations. What is

acceptable by the customer or project sponsor?
- What is the acceptable tolerance of error? – Benchmarking – Compare actual with planned project practices.
- Plan how the following scientific methods may be used to gather more information on produced quality:
  - Design of Experiment – To identify factors that may affect the resulting product or process of the project.
  - Statistical Sampling – Randomly picking from result to measure quality.
- Apply other methods such as:
  - Brainstorming
  - Force field Analysis
  - Nominal Group Technique
  - Quality Management and Control Tools – Link and sequence identified activities.

  - Follow the structure PMI® approach of planning:
    - Perform Cost-Benefit Analysis
    - Evaluate the Cost of Quality – Cost of conformance to quality versus the cost of nonconformance.
    - Use the basic 7 quality tools for performing quality within the plan-do-check-act context:
      - Cause-and-effect diagrams
      - Flowcharts
      - Check-sheets
      - Pareto diagrams
      - Histograms
      - Control Charts
      - Scatter diagrams

- ❖ **Perform Quality Assurance** - This is the auditing of the work done against the defined quality standards and requirements. It ensures that quality plan is followed through in the project, a change request approach is followed, and perform integrated change control is followed per requirement:

91

- *Do the right things* - To ensure that review takes place and the right resources take part in the review process.
- *Do things better* - Review the quality assurance process.
- *Are we doing it right* - continuous process improvement—the root cause analysis.
- *Why are errors in the project* – Audit and use quality metrics for measurement. The audit is usually carried out by external body to ensure no bias in measuring project against project policies, processes and procedures.
- *Use available tools to perform quality assurance*
    - **Affinity Diagrams** – Decompose and taxonomically organize work to be done.
    - **Process decision program charts (PDPC)** – Facilitate contingency planning using hierarchical breakdown of work to be done.
    - **Interrelationship diagraphs** – Determine the relationships between the works represented in previous diagrams and pictorially represent the logical sequence of events.
    - **Tree diagrams** – Commonly used for WBS, RBS (Risk Breakdown Structure) and OBS (Organization Breakdown Structure). A decision tree that displays vertically or horizontally the parent to child relationship, or top-down decomposition of problem into simpler manageable tasks.
    - **Prioritization Matrices** – Consolidate all relevant project requirements and issues; rank them in order of importance for implementation.
    - **Activity Network diagrams** – These are activity diagram described in Time management. Activity on Node (AON) or Activity on Arrow (AOA).
    - **Matrix diagrams** – A spreadsheet format data analysis to derive factors, causes and objectives.

❖ **Control Quality** - This is to ensure that we are doing the right thing and delivering the right results. To perform quality

control, follow these steps:
- Perform quality control measurement.
- Make recommendation for changes.
- Validate changes.
- Validate deliverables.
- The resulting product is fit to use. Business requirements are met by the results.
- Deliverable is inspected, measured, and tested.
- Process of quality control includes inspection, testing, sampling, and statistical control.

Other Related Quality Standards

- **Total Quality Management (TQM)** - A quality management process that requires all individual in the company to be responsible for quality, shifts quality from product to process of producing products, and focuses on improvement in process and results.

- **International Standard Organization (ISO)** - A voluntary, non-treaty federation of standards setting bodies of some 130 countries. Founded in 1946-47 in Geneva as a UN agency, it promotes development of standardization and related activities to facilitate international trade in goods and services and cooperation on economic, intellectual, scientific, and technological aspects. (Source: *www.businessdictionary.com*) ISO 9000—A standard for performing quality assurance with emphasis on the following:
    - Customer Satisfactions
    - Prevention over inspection
    - Continuous Improvement using plan-do-check-act approach such as CMMI
    - Management Responsibility
    - Cost of quality (COQ)

- **Six Sigma** - Six Sigma seeks to improve the quality of process outputs by identifying and removing the causes of defects (errors) and minimizing variability in manufacturing and business processes. It uses a set of quality management methods, including statistical methods, and creates a special infrastructure of people within the organization ("Black Belts," "Green Belts," etc.) who are experts in these methods. (Source: http://en.wikipedia.org)

- **Juran Crosby Deming**
    - *Crosby*—It is conformance to requirements, not as goodness. It is management's job to set the requirements and communicate to employees.
    - *Deming*—Meeting and exceeding the customer's need and expectations and then continuing to improve.
    - *Juran*—Quality mission of the company is "fitness for use" as perceived by customers. The missions of individual departments are to work according to specifications designed to achieve fitness for use.
- **KAIZEN (Continuous Improvement)** - Japanese management term.
    - Constant process improvement.
- **Just-in-Time (JIT)** - A production strategy that strives to improve a business' return on investment by reducing in-process inventory and associated carrying costs.
    - Zero or near zero inventory
    - Focuses on quality
    - No excess inventory

Why prevention should be emphasized in quality plan
- Prevention is keeping defects from occurring in the project.
- Inspection is catching errors that have occurred in the results of the project.
- It is cheaper to fix issues at prevention level.

- Fixes are costly at inspection level.
- See graph below:

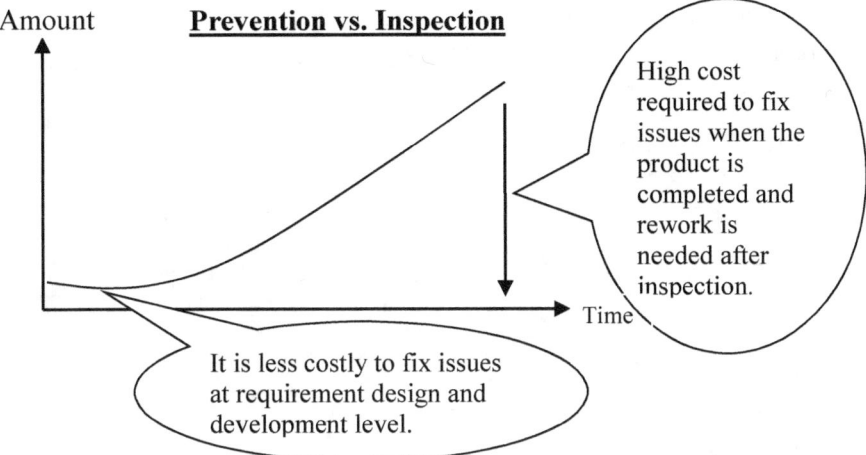

Figure 16: Prevention & Inspection Chart.

Methods of Quality Control

- **Cause and Effect Diagram (Ishikawa Diagram or Fishbone Diagram)** — This is a method of determining the effect of various factors on a potential problem. The diagram provides visibility to potential cause of a problem:

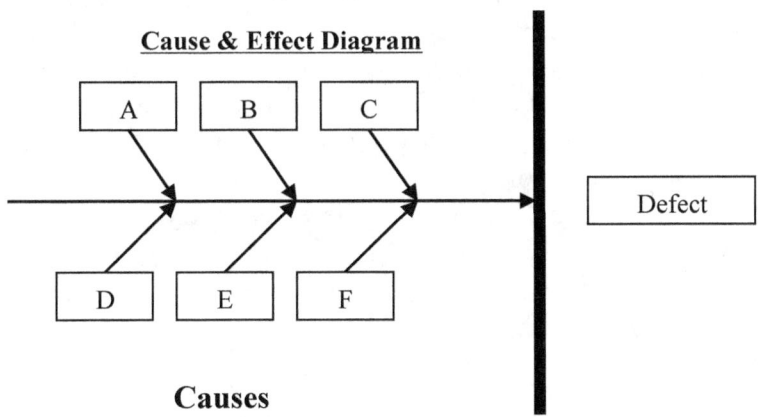

Figure 17: Cause & Effect Chart.

- **Pareto Chart** - This is the application of the 80/20 rule.

Generally used to identify and evaluate nonconformities. The 80% of the problems are due to 20% of the causes. Fix the 20% of the problems that are major hits due to time constraints because the majority of the problems are within the 20%. The 80% of our time is spent fixing A, B, C (20%).

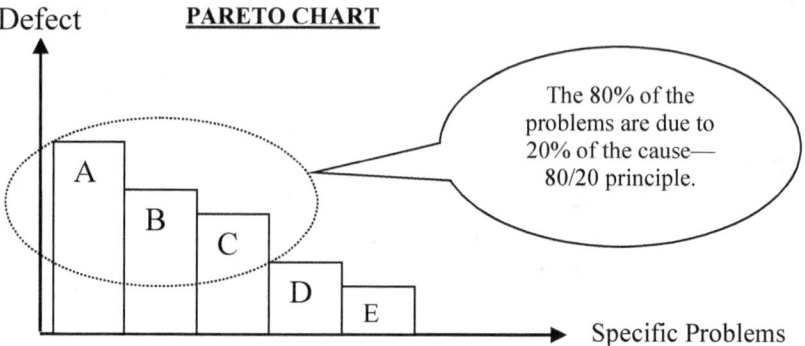

Figure 18: Pareto Chart.

- **Control Charts** - Control charts are for monitoring project and product life cycle process. Control charts are for determining the stability and predictable performance on a project or product life cycle process. The steps for using control charts include the following:
    - Establish the midpoint for measuring the success of the project.
    - Plot measurements to make sure projects are within the limits of quality.
    - Take corrective actions to bring project back to midpoint.
    - Use the rule of 7 where necessary.

Figure 19: Control Chart.

- **Standard Deviation (Six Sigma)**—Standard deviation is used to set quality levels and control limits.

Figure 20: Standard Deviation Chart.

- The following defines the steps of Six Sigma:
    o It uses bell curve.
    o Most organizations aim for Six Sigma.
    o Use Six Sigma to refine the quality process.
    o Use the appropriate sigma level base on time and money.

- **Tolerance versus Control Limits**—Tolerance is the acceptable limit set for product quality. Control limits are acceptable variances in project or product life cycle process.

The following diagram shows a process operating within a 3-sigma control limits.

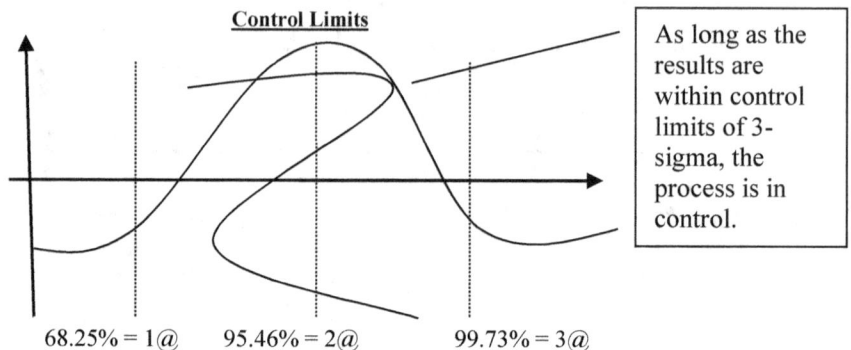

Figure 21: Control Limits Chart.

- Other quality control tools include as follows:
    - Benchmarking—The measurement of project results against previous projects.
    - Run Charts — It shows the history and pattern of variations.
    - Scatter Diagrams—It shows the pattern of relationship between control variables.
    - Sampling
        - Statistical Sampling—Random sampling of products to minimize overall quality control measurement costs.
        - Variable Sampling— Measuring precision or closeness to quality conformance.
        - Attribute Sampling—Product either conforms to quality or it does not. Discreet measurement method—one or zero, 100% or 0.
            - **Inspection** - The examination of product for quality conformance.
            - **Defect Review** - This could be peer review or management review of deliverable defects.

Per PMI® standards, project quality management expects

project manager to deliver what has been promised and only what has been promised in the project scope. There should be no gold plating. Do not deliver more than what has been promised to avoid compromising quality that will be delivered.

Chapter 15: Project Resource Management

Project resource management is the process to identify, acquire and manage resources needed for a project. The resources include team and physical resources. The team resources require soft skills and the need for project managers to develop a style for dealing with project team, human resources, vendors and stakeholders. A method personalized for dealing with team motivation, conflict resolution, support, and interacting with team members, vendors and stakeholders. It may be necessary for the project manager to deliver a style of project management consistent to his or her personality. The key attributes to remember when performing this role are:

- Influencing the project team and all relevant stakeholders relatively to the environment, communication, politics, cultural, geographical and organizational practice and structure.
- Acting professionally, practicing and promoting good ethical behavior on the project.
- Promoting collaboration and supportive environment through delegation of decisions to team members.
- Adapting the relevant resource management method relative to the project and the environment. Popular methods adapted over the years include:
    - Lean Management – Kanban
    - Just-In-Time – JIT
    - Kaizen
    - Total Productive Management – TPM
    - Theory of Constraints – TOC
    - Scrum/Agile Approach

- Apply emotional intelligence (EI) for self-management and awareness and improve relationship to foster effective bonding on the project.
- Provide team with environment and support needed to foster self-organization. The team is able to function without central control watching over the team.
- Virtual teams/distributed may be applied to depending efficient use of your organization resources. This method requires effective communication means amongst the teams.

The physical resources management involves managing the physical resources like servers, computers, materials, building etc. for a project. The identification, acquisition and management are under this process.

The following are the processes in project resources management:

- ❖ **Plan Resource Management** – This is the planning of efficient and effective deployment of resources as needed on a project. This consist of defining how to estimate, acquire, manage and utilize team and physical resources. The planning is documented as requirement for the different (team and physical) resources needed on the project. The plan should include the level of skills required for the areas of work in the project for team resources. Similar details, such as high-level description of physical resource must also be specified in the plan. For example, we need two servers to support our disaster recovery project. The following should be considered when developing the resource management plan:
    - o **Team Resource**
        - o Participate in formal or informal networking events in the organization to facilitate the planning and selection of resources.
        - o Apply knowledge of organizational theory in creating human resource plan. These theories include:
            - Maslow Hierarchy of needs
            - McGregor's Theory X and Y Theory
            - Contingency Theory
            - See develop project team section of this chapter

on theories of people behaviors:
- Define the needed skills.
- Define when the resources are needed on the project.
- Define the number of skilled analyst required.
- Define how long the resources are needed on the project.
- Provide a transition plan if necessary.
- Provide a staff rotation plan if necessary.
- Define the level of authority required in the project.
- Conduct meetings and apply expert judgment to ensure that the plan for human resources will be effective and accepted by all respective parties.

- **Develop Project Org Chart.** Draw the organization chart to show reporting structure. Draw both the project and the organization charts to understand the possible conflicts, career aspirations, relationships between management structures:

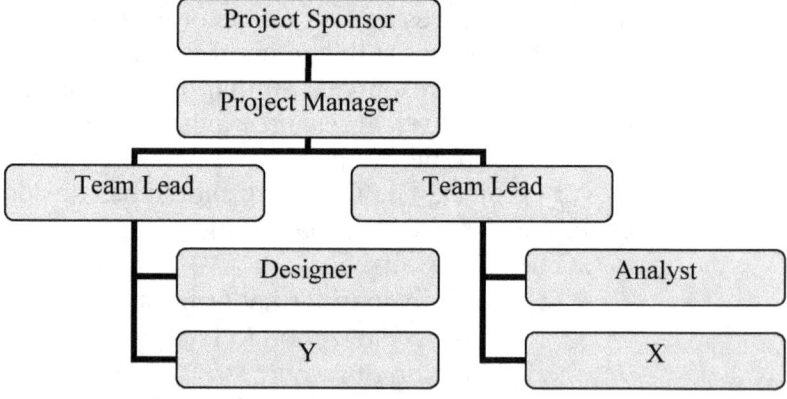

Figure 22: Project Org Chart.

- **Define Roles and Responsibilities.** Define the roles and responsibilities for the following resources, decision makers, escalation levels, etc.:
  - Project manager.
  - Stakeholders.

- o Senior management. They will be accepting the final deliverables, etc.
- o Sponsor/acceptor.
- o Functional manager.
- o Team for status reporting.
- o RACI matrix is a chart for the illustration of the roles and responsibilities on a project. RACI stands for **R**esponsible **A**ccountable **C**onsult **I**nform. This may also be referred to as RAM, **R**esponsibility **A**ssignment **M**atrix.
- **Physical Resource**
  - o Define the physical resources needed for the project. C
  - o Inspect internally so see what resources are available within the organization's assets.
  - o Solicit for vendors on needed materials.
  - o Follow your procurement process to acquire physical resources.
  - o Manage and utilize the physical resources per project requirement.

❖ Estimate Activity Resources
- o Use the project scope, project blueprint, and work breakdown structure, available resource calendar, risk register, cost of resources, and organization policies to determine the following:
  - The needed resources from goods, supplies or materials and people standpoints.
  - The quantities of resources needed on the project.
  - When are the resources needed?
- o Methods for estimating activity resources include:
  - Expert judgment based on experience.
  - Make or buy analysis of alternatives.
  - General research on industry published data relating to the project.

- Bottom-Up estimation by summation from the lowest component of WBS to the top the structure.
- Use available software tools, such as Microsoft Project.
- Measure against Productivity metrics

❖ **Acquire Project Team.** This is the staffing of project with the type of resources described in the project management plan. If experiencing challenges in staffing project due to lack of required resources, make changes in the human resources plan to accommodate the challenges.
  o Develop staff assignment.
  o Develop resource calendar.
  o Negotiate with respective bodies to acquire the required resources.
  o Consider alternative resources to achieve project objectives but stay within agreement or regulations. Virtual team or less qualified resources may be considered as alternative resources.

❖ **Develop Project Team.** The project manager has the responsibility to develop a team for the project to be delivered on time, on budget to project scope. The following should be provided to the project team:
  o Training
  o Ground rules—Formal and informal rules that defines the boundaries on the project.
  o Team building activities. – Manage the project team through the Forming, Storming, Norming, Performing and Adjourning phases of team building while working through the project process groups.
  o Interpersonal skills (soft skills).
  o Collocates of resources or create war room on project site to enhance performance of resources.
  o Motivation using recognition and reward theories—These theories include the following:
    - **Maslow Hierarchy of Needs** - The lower needs must be satisfied before people can reach their upper needs using

the following hierarchy from Abraham Maslow:

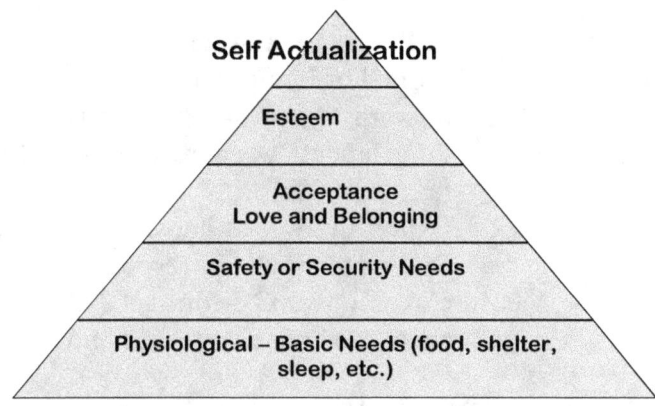

Figure 23: Maslow Hierarchy.

- **McGregor's Theory X and Y Theory**
    - Theory X—People are lazy by default. They need constant supervision to achieve desire result.
    - Theory Y—People are motivated naturally to do good work.
- **Herzberg** - The presence of certain factor does not make staff satisfied. But lack of it will dissatisfy the staff.

- **Contingency Theory**
    - The effectiveness of a leader is dependent on whether the leader is task oriented or relationship oriented.
    - Situational Factors—Task oriented is more suitable for stressful environment. But a balance in human relationship may also be needed for the success of the project.

- **McClelland's Three-Need Theory** - The achievement

theory.
-
  - The desire for achievement. High achievers group together.
  - The desire for power. Social or individual power.
  - The desire for affiliation (with a team).

- **Forms of Project Manager Power**
  - Formal or Legitimate - Due by position.
  - Reward - Motivate with a reward.
  - Punishment - A coercive power if goal is not met by team member.
  - Expert - Power of knowledge on a subject.
  - Referent - Power of respect and personality.
- Measure overall team performance after applying the development methods mentioned above.

❖ **Manage Project Team** - The project manager has the responsibility to coordinate project team, track team member, and project performance, manage project changes, and resolve any conflicts. Specific methods to be used by project manager are as follows:
- **Observation and Conversation** - Manage day-to-day project activities by working with team members on status update, monitoring progress, and communicating on any pending issues.
- **Project Performance Appraisal** - Appraise individuals on their job performance on the project.
- **Manage Conflicts** - Encourage positive project working environment by resolving conflicts as they surface on the project. The following are known methods for resolving conflicts and roles recognition that facilitates the ability to resolve the conflicts:
- **Conflict Resolution Methods**
  - **Problem Solving (Confrontation)**— Recommended by PMI® group to be the best approach because it involves addressing the conflict head-on to a resolution. Address the issue, *not* the

person.
- **Compromise** - A lose-lose approach to resolve the conflict. A deadlock situation resolution.
- **Forcing** - The use of force to resolve conflict is generally least accepted. It may reduce morale on the project and damaging in the long term.
- **Smoothing** - This is an attempt to diminish the problem. It is not really solved but may be appropriate for certain situation.
- **Withdrawal** - This is an avoidance approach with the hope that the problem will go away.

- **Role Types**
- **Constructive Roles**
  - Initiator—Thinker
  - Encourager—Motivator
  - Information seeker
  - Information giver
  - Clarifiers
  - Harmonizers
  - Summarizers
  - Gatekeepers
  - Director
- **Destructive Roles**
  - Aggressors
  - Blockers
  - Withdrawers
  - Recognition seekers
  - Topic jumpers
  - Dominator
  - Devil's advocate

- **Control Resources**: This is the process that ensures that resources are available as planned for the project. The process monitors the availability and usage of resources to ensure actual utilization is as planned. Where there is deviation from the planned usage, corrective action is taken to stay within planned. Resources are released when no longer needed as part of the control process.

The project manager must determine his or her personality and balance hard and soft skills to effectively manage a project. Experience has revealed that individuals are generally not in favor of being managed because change in behavior is required. Project managers should focus on managing the project work and not exactly the people. A work-life balance for the resources on the project should be maintained. This will help to encourage supportive and creative resources instead of robots waiting for the next order.

Chapter 16: Project Communication Management

Project communication management is the coordination processes for planning, creating, gathering, management, control, storage and retrieval of information to be distributed on a project. This process group also ensures timely, appropriate and effective communication of project information on the project. The processes included in the project communication management include the following:

- ❖ **Plan communication.** This is the planning process to determine project information base on stakeholders' requirements, and how the information will be distributed to the respective parties. The communication management plan consist of the following:
    - The frequency of communication distribution and
    - The format of communication or communication techniques.
    - **Style of Communication**
        - Interactive — Two or multiple-way communication.
        - Pull — Request for status or feedback.
        - Push — Announce or presenting information.
        - Encrypted or non-encrypted information for sharing.
    - **Methods of Communication**
        - **Informal Written**
            - Memos and e-mails—Type professional-looking e-mail that delivers the right message.
        - **Formal Written**
            - Reports
            - Contracts
            - Legal document

- Project document
- Project Websites—Develop simple project websites to help organize project
- **Informal Verbal**
  - In person
  - Instant messengers
  - Phone calls
  - Meetings
  - Discussions
- **Formal Verbal**
  - Presentations—good quality presentation, professional
  - Conference calls
  - Speeches
  - Mass communication
- **What information to distribute:**
  - Status—The good and bad news of the project status.
  - Plan Updates—Change management. Implementing **changes** to the project.
  - Team Performance—Time spent on tasks from team members. Status report from team members.
  - Meetings—A well-managed meeting can be very effective for project communication.
  - Problems—The project communication must be open to problem communication from stakeholders, team members, and project manager.
  - Which stakeholder will receive information?
    - Stakeholder Register—List of identified risks.
- A template for the communication plan should contain at least the following:
  - Communication Requirement
  - Format, language and description.
  - Purpose of distribution
  - Frequency and Time frame of information

- distribution.
  - Approval list of stakeholders for the information to be distributed, inclusive of who will be receiving the information.
  - Who is responsible for communicating the information?
  - Method of communication.
  - Information flow chart for the organization
  - Constraints and Assumptions.

- ❖ **Manage Communications** – This is an executing process of organizing the creation, collection, distribution, storing and retrieval of information for a project based on the communication plan. The specific methods that can be used to manage communication includes:
  - Sender-Receiver Models
  - Choice of Media – Oral or written communication?
  - Writing Style – Formal or Informal writing
  - Meeting Management – Formal meetings
  - Presentation Technique – Visual aids and body language.
  - Facilitation Techniques – Workshop session
  - Listening Technique – List an ask questing question t clarify understand
  - The expected output from manage communication includes:
    - Update to Project management plan
    - Update to project documents such as requirement, issue log, schedule, and design or implementation documentation updates.
    - New communication with stakeholders.
    - Project report and related documentations, including status and lesson learned.
    - Feedbacks and lesson learned.

- ❖ **Report Performance** - This is a management communication process to gather details on project requirements or expectations and report on what has been delivered for performance measurement. The following are some of the information to be reported:

- Project weekly status.
- Project monthly status.
- Progress and milestones—consolidated team status report.
- Stakeholder management.
- Consistency—To be consistent in the status report delivery, issues and meetings status reporting.

❖ **Control Communications** – This is the monitoring and controlling of project communication to meet the requirements of stakeholders. Control communication ensures project information is optimally distributed throughout the life of the project. The control of communication may be based on the following in the project:
  - Project Status Reports.
  - Schedules.
  - Cost incurred to date.
  - Issue Log.
  - Performance feedback on or off the project.
  - Available organization assets.

The control of communication on the project can be exercised by performing the following:
- **Using available IT tools** such as email, Microsoft projects, Power Point and Word document. Use whatever is provided by your organization.
- **Conduct meetings** to discuss project, issues, requirements, and all project related matters to facilitate quick resolution of matters.
- **Use experience and expert** judgment to determine that the right message is communicated to the right audience, at the right time. The services of consultants, subject matter expert, and other external professional bodies may be employed for expert judgment.

Communication Channel

As part of analyzing communication requirement and determining which stakeholder should receive project communication, it is required that the communication channel and the path of communication should be determined:

$$\text{Communication Channels} = [n \times (n-1)]/2$$

Communication Model

Further analysis into the communication requirement is the communication model. Messages are conveyed in sender-receiver model, and to ensure that they are conveyed correctly. It is necessary to study the receiver's response to the sent messages. Encoded messages are transmitted via a medium to a receiver, an acknowledge message request is sent by the receiver to sender. A feedback message is sent back to the sender. The following are the models of communication commonly used:

- **Active Listening** - The receiver of message constantly indicates successful reception and comprehension of message.
- **Effective Listening** - Similar to active listening. Indicate with vocal or body language the understanding of message received with full attention to sender's message.
- **Feedback** - Receiver constantly provides feedback on message received, whether it is understood or unclear.
- **Nonverbal** - Constant indication with body language on the clarity of message received.
- **Para lingual** - These are vocal signs to indicate receiver's attention to messages being received from sender. Pitch and tone of voice are used for this process.

Chapter 17: Project Risk Management

Project risk management is the management of processes that identify and analyze risks, risk response planning, monitors and controls factors contributing to risks on a project. It involves dealing with the unknowns; but the objective is to mitigate risk on a project. The project risk management consists of the following processes:

- ❖ **Plan Risk Management** - This is the process of developing strategies for dealing with risk or managing risk. Creating an overall plan for risk management. The risk management plan should include the following:
    - o **Executive Summary** - An overall strategy for managing risk on the project. The objective of the project as described in the project charter and a detailed analysis of stakeholders' openness to risks will help in defining the executive summary:
        - What is the project description, requirements and the associated *high-level risks*? Is this defined in the project charter?
        - Are *stakeholders* (including project sponsor) risk seekers or avoiders? High-profile projects are generally risk avoiders because of the project cost.
        - *Corporate factors* - Is this risk-taking corporate environment or risk-avoidance organization? There may be resistance if the strategy does not go along with the corporate strategy.
        - *Risk Management Approach or Strategy* - The process or approach to be followed in identifying risk on the project and managing the risks. How

rigorous is risk management on the project?
- *History/Experience* — Based organization or project history, build into the plan the risk profile. This should help to define the approach for managing risk on the project.
  - **Methodology** – What approach will be used to tackle risk? This question plus the tools and data sources to be used for risk management must the defined in the plan.
  - **Roles and Responsibilities of Stakeholders** - Define the roles and responsibilities of stakeholders in managing risks. Who is responsible for risk management on the project?
  - **Categorization of Risk** – Risk can be categorized using the Risk Breakdown Structure, which is a step for identifying all possible sources of risks on the project. An example of how to break down the risks is as follows:
    - **Level 0** - Project Risks
      - **Level 1** – Technical Risks
        - **Level 2** – Document risks details from Scope, requirements, processes, technology and interfaces standpoints.
      - **Level 1 – Management Risks**
        - **Level 2** – Document risks impact from program/project, operations, organization, resources and communications standpoints.
      - **Level 1 – Commercial Risks**
        - **Level 2** – Document contractual, procurement, supplier, vendors, customer and partnership impacts.
      - **Level 1 – External Risks**
        - **Level 2** – Document risks from external factors that may impact the project. Such factors include legislation, exchange or interest rate, facilities, environmental, weather, competition, regulations etc.

- **Scaling of Risk** – Risk can be further categorized base on level of impact. It enables addressing the risks in their order of impact. Rate risk on scale of low, medium, or high based on probabilities and impact assessments. High risks are dealt with followed by medium risks, then low-rated risks.
  - **Budgeting** - Budget for the risk measures in the project cost baseline.
  - **Risk Probabilities and Impact** - This is the qualitative analysis of risk to measure the different levels of risk probabilities and impact on the project. The result of this assessment is included in the risk management plan for project references.

❖ **Identify Risks** - Risks are components to the events that involve uncertainties or unplanned activities. Risks may affect a project positively, reducing the cost and time of a project, or negatively increasing cost and time. Risk identification is an iterative process that deals with how unknown risks or uncertainties are identified and documented as risk register. The project management plan, scope, and other environmental factors are considered when identifying the risks on a project:

  - **Factors to be considered when identifying risks**:
    - **Known Risk** - For example, training is needed for the deployment of a new system. There may be some issues after deployment because training is required. Time and money may be required for training.
    - **Unknown Risks** - Allocate additional time and money for unknown risks. Contingency is required. Create funding for the known and unknown risks (contingency funds).
    - **Source of Risk** - The following are possible source of risk on the project:
      - **Technology Risk** - Known and unknown technology issues, money, and time allocation.

- Team—How corporative is the team? More risks with less corporative team.
- Scope—Loosely defined scope means more risk.
- Business—How stable is the business?
- Economy—Good or bad economy?
- Competition—Is company leading competition a possible higher risk?

  o If the PMI® process is strictly followed, the following will help in identifying risk on the project:
  - **Risk Management Plan** – A comprehensive plan will contain, roles & responsibilities, budget, schedule, risk categorization and risk breakdown structure. These items will help in identifying risk on the project.
  - **Cost Management Plan** – Cost control process as defined in the plan can help to identify risks.
  - **Schedule Management Plan** – Specific activities and project time to be affected by risk can be studied and mitigated.
  - **Quality Management Plan** – Deviation from baseline of quality measures and metrics is a risk. Use the plan to determine risk points on the project.
  - **Human Resources Management Plan** – Inability to meet the set plan for human resources on skill sets required on a project is a risk. Measure conformance to the plan.
  - **Scope Baseline** – Track project risks from assumptions, through WBS to work package level.
  - **Activity Cost Estimation** – Exercise risk quantitative analysis using cost estimated for the WBS.
  - **Activity Duration Estimation** – Analyze risk based on duration of activity laid out for the project. Add buffer for task where necessary to meet overall project goals.

- **Procurement** – What are the activities and cost to meet procurement requirements? Measure risk associated procurement of needed resources.

- **Risk Identification Techniques** - What techniques are available to this project?
    - **Brainstorming** - Set up a team or brainstorming session to identify all possible or probable risks on the project.
    - **Delphi Technique** - Use project experts on the project to identify risks based on their experience.
    - **Interviews** - Interview individuals, businesses, and stakeholders on project to identify the risk factors that can affect the success of the project.
    - **Root Cause Analysis** - Apply root because analysis or the Ishikawa diagram to drill down in detail into project risks.
    - **SWOT Analysis** - Strength, Weakness, Opportunities, and Threats analysis of project based on experience.
    - **Checklist Analysis** – Use checklist to mitigate risk. The checklist is developed based on similar project experience.
    - **Assumptions Analysis** – All support assumptions must be examined to ensure accuracy since project progress is based on them.
    - **Diagramming** – Pictorial analysis of risk using any of the following method or as applicable:
        - Cause and effect diagrams
        - System or Process Flowcharts
        - Influence Diagrams

❖ **Qualitative Risk** - This is the ranking and prioritization of risks identified on a project based on their probability level of impacting the project. The project organization can focus on high-priority risks that will impact timeline while lower priority risks are addressed as time and cost permit on the project. To facilitate qualitative risk analysis is the probability and impact matrix used for risk assessment based on cost, time, scope, and quality. The following table is a format for the **probability and impact matrix**:

Project Objective	Low (1)	Medium (3)	High (7)	Very High (9)
Cost	Insignificant	<5%	<10%	>10%
Time	Insignificant	<10 days	<25days	>25days
Scope	Insignificant	No business Impact	Some business problems	Definite business impact
Quality	Insignificant	No anticipated problems	Potential Line Problems	Definite Problems
Result	Low			
Ranking	Cost < 5% (Medium) Time>27days (High)			

Other methods for performing qualitative risk analysis include:
- **Risk Data Quality Assessment** – Evaluating the accuracy, quality, reliability and integrity of the data available for risk assessment. Ensure that reliable data is used for risk assessment.

- **Risk Categorization** – Use expert judgment to categorize risks per work packages, project phases and activities. Facilitate responses and quick identification of risky project areas.

- **Risk Urgency Assessment** – Address high priority risks urgently with quick and near-term responses. The probability and impact matrix are good inputs for this task.

- ❖ **Quantitative Analysis** - This process focuses on numerically qualifying project risks to identify those that need the most attention because of their impact on the project timeline. The purpose of quantitative risk analysis includes the following:

- Analysis of risks that have be qualitatively analyzed.
- Analysis of high-impact risks - These are risks that require high money value.
- Numeric rating of risks - Quantify risk in money value.
- Measure overall and aggregate effect of project risks before and after responses have been applied on the project.
- Risk impact simulation - A technique such as Monte Carlo simulation software may be used for this analysis and calculation.
- Decision Tree - A decision tree may be drawn as shown to determine shower down impact. The following example shows the cost impact of price increase on the equipment required to deploy a project, and the cost impact of not providing training on the new system to be deployed:

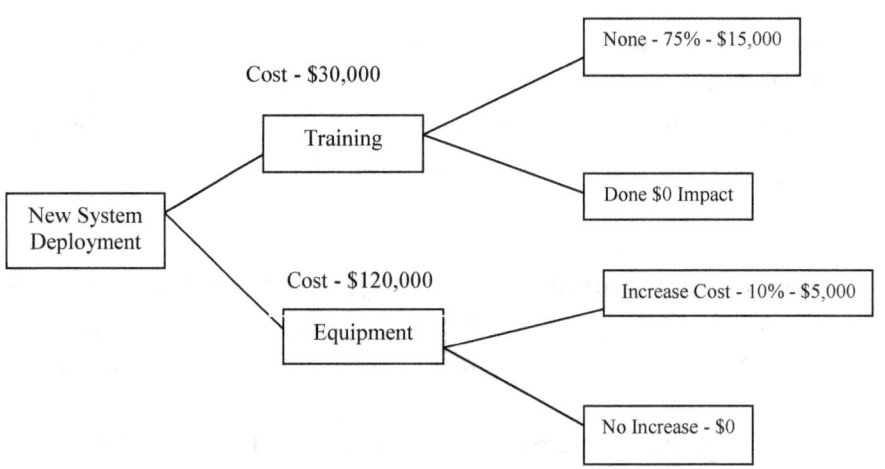

Figure 24: Decision Tree.

- The following table is the numerical analysis of the decision tree:
-

	Initial Cost	Risk Cost	Probability	Total
Training	$30,000.00	$15,000.00	75%	$30,000.00 + ($15,000.00 x 75%) = $41,250.00
Equipment	$120,000.00	$5,000.00	10%	$120,000.00 + ($5000 x 10%) = $120,500.00

- Training requires a minimum contingency amount of $41,250.00.
- Equipment requires a minimum contingency amount of $120,500.00.

Other methods that could be applied to quantitatively analysis include:
- **Interviewing** – Utilize expert experience and historical information to quantify risk for probability and impact risk analysis.
- **Probability Analysis** – Utilize probability distributions to represent uncertainties in project costs and durations to measure risk.

- **Sensitivity Analysis** – Examine each risk identified and quantified, then determine which one has the most effect on the project with any little variations. Tornado diagram is an example of sensitivity analysis.

- **Expected Monetary Value Analysis** – Calculates the average outcome of a project using conditional future (probability) values that may or may never occur. Opportunities from future occurrence results to positive values, while threats result to negative EMV values.

- **Modelling and Simulation** – This is the iterative computation of project model using random values from cost estimates, durations, and their probability distribution for cost risk and schedule risk analysis respectively. This is Monte Carlo technique.

- ❖ **Plan Risk Response** - This is the process of planning how all the analyzed risk in the risk registered will be managed or handled. Planning ahead of time on how threats will be eliminated or probabilities of threats will be decreased and increasing the probabilities of opportunities on the project. The plan should include clearly defined strategies for threats and opportunities.
  - o **Strategies for threats are as follows**:
    - *Avoid*. Change the project plan, scope, schedule, requirements and strategies or objectives to remove threats completely from the project.
    - *Transfer*. Insurance—Transfer risk to a third party at a cost or contract out project to qualified contractor or external firm.
    - *Mitigate*. What can you do to lessen the impact of a risk? Risk cannot be eliminated but can be lessen to an acceptable threshold limit. Provide training to minimize risk but provide contingency plan to cover risk just in case.
    - *Accept*. There are some project risks that you may have to just accept. Put a contingency amount and/or time to accept contingency risk.
  - o **Strategies for opportunities include the following:**
    - *Exploit*. Change project management plan to ensure opportunity occur. For example, project may be completed earlier before the plan date. Add more resources to exploit opportunity.
    - *Share*. Government project might require prime contractors to partner with small businesses to win government contracts. Partner with small businesses to achieve the positive risk or opportunity of winning large government contracts.
    - *Enhance*. Do not mitigate risk here but increase the probability of the risk or opportunity.
    - *Accept*. This also applies to opportunities. The

sudden discovery of training requirement for unplanned system or business activity. Training can be a source of revenue for the organization.
  - All relevant **project management plans are updated** to reflect changes made due to response for risk planning.

- ❖ **Implement Risk Responses**
  This is the implementation of risk response agreed for the risks on the project. The responses are executed as planned to mitigate risks, minimize threats to the project and maximize the opportunities from the project. The risk responses are defined based on several factors including:
  - Lesson learned from previous projects.
  - Project management plan
  - Available Assets
  - Expert judgment
  - Team and Soft skills
  - Cost
  - Time

- ❖ **Monitor Risks**
  This is the process of monitoring the implementation of the planned risk responses to control project. The purposes of this process are as follows:
  - **Monitor known risks**
    - **Risk Register** - Track the status of risks listed in the risk register. Monitor the risks per timeline and deal with the risks that are near timeline. The following is a sample risk register table:

Risk Register				
Risk Item	Probability Impact	Risk Management Strategy	Critical Dates	Current Status
Inadequate Training	Medium	Mitigate	This Week	No Issues
Increase Equipment Prices	High	Accept	This month	Review Periodically

- **Monitor Risk Profile**—Monitor risks based on the

information in the risk profile to mitigate the impact of the risks. High-profile risks are of high urgency, or high-impact risk should receive more focus.

- o **Assess Risks** - Look out for new risk in the following:
    - Scope changes—Monitor scope changes and impact on schedule and cost.
    - Schedule changes—Monitor schedule changes due to new risks.
    - Environment changes—Monitor impact of environmental changes.
    - Interview project stakeholders.

- o **Manage Contingency** - Ensure fund allocated for contingency are spent only on the risk.
- o **Audit Risks** - Audit the overall risk management process to ensure that risk is properly managed on the project.
- o **Status Meetings** - Hold frequent status meetings to discuss status.
- o **Variance & Trend Analysis** – Use trend analysis to compare planned results to the actual results on costing and schedule. Earned valued analysis is a good example.
- o **Technical Performance Management** – Compare planned or expected technical performance to actuals from implementation execution.

The output from this process includes:
- List of corrective Actions
- List of preventive actions
- Updates of the relevant plans affected by risk planning.

Risk is inevitable in every project. It is important that they are managed at their early stage within the context of PMI® standard and policies of the organization.

Chapter 18: Procurement Management

Procurement management is management of processes to acquire and purchase goods and services required for the project. Depending on the scale of the purchase, a contract may be produced, which ensures that the sellers and buyers have legally binding documents that detail the legal requirements of the transactions.

The project procurement management processes are the following:

- ❖ **Plan Procurement** - The purpose of this process is to plan purchases, acquisitions, and the type of contracts to be used for transaction. The following are the steps to be taken during plan procurement:
    o Make or buy decision. Make the product or services as part of the project. Decide on buy decision as part of the procurement process.
    o Plan and decide on how much to buy.
    o When to buy the product and services. Timely purchase.
    o Decide on the type of contract (how much control do you want on the project procurement process):
        ▪ Fixed Price Contract
        ▪ Firm Fixed Price
        ▪ Fixed Price Incentive Fee (FPIF)
        ▪ Fixed Price Economic Price Adjustment (FP-EPA)
            • Time and Material
            • Cost Reimbursable Contracts
            • Cost Plus Fixed Fee (CPFF)
            • Cost Plus Incentive Fee (CPIF)

- Plan the details of the selected contract.
- Prepare for Request for Proposal (RFP)/Request for Information (RFI)/Request for Quotation (RFQ).
- Define the scope of the proposal.
- No ambiguity in the contract details.
  - Create Statement of Work (SOW) for the product or service to be purchased.
  - Create selection criteria for the vendors to be selected.

❖ **Conduct Procurement** - This is the process that executes the activities defined in the procurement management plan. This process evaluates potential sellers and seller's responses. The following are the activities to be executed during the conduct procurement process:
- Qualified sellers must be in the organization procurement system. Evaluate only the qualifying vendors in the system.
- Conduct bidders' conference.
- Issue request to qualified vendors.
- Evaluate seller proposals based on available resources such as experts and independent research of expected proposal content.
- Request seller's response.
- Evaluate responses.
  - Use the evaluation sheet.
  - Multiple evaluators.
  - Technical requirement (best).
  - Financial requirements (best).
  - Reference.
    - Rank the vendors.
      - Produce the final contract.
    - Legal documentation—Engage the legal department for the terms and conditions defined in the contract.
    - The project manager must look closely into the scope statements, functions—all that is needed to support the project and as defined in the SOW:
      - Award contract. Award the contract to the most qualified vendor as determined from the proposal evaluation.

- ❖ **Control Procurement** - This is the management of contracts between the buyer and seller to ensure that the content agreed upon in the contract is delivered according to the terms defined in the contract. Administrative activities during this process include the following:
    - Management of contract compliance.
    - Terms and conditions of the contract must not be violated.
    - Monitor the terms and conditions of the project.
    - Monitor term changes.
        - Payments systems.
    - To ensure that amount paid is as defined in the contract.
    - To ensure that payment is paid per the schedule defined in the contract.
    - The term and conditions of payment must be followed.
        - Change management and control of the contract contents.
    - A change management process must be in place to change the contract.
    - Any deviation from terms and conditions must be managed in the contract.
    - Manage to the exact terms of the contract.
        - Manage project performance with respect to the expectations defined in the contract.

Chapter 19: Project Stakeholder Management

Stakeholder management is the coordination of processes required to identify stakeholders (people, organizations and groups) of the project, communicate, understand and manage their expectations. The stakeholders are people, organizations and groups that have direct or special interest in the project. The processes required to manage stakeholders' satisfaction include the following:

- ❖ **Identify Stakeholders.** This is an initiating process. It involves identifying all the respective stakeholders that will be affected positively or negatively by the implementation of this project.
    - o This is usually done when compiling the project charter. This of stakeholders should in the **project charter**.
    - o **Procurement documents** – The selected vendors with established contracts are stakeholders.
    - o **Other** factors for stakeholders identification include :
        - Culture and structure
        - History or Assets – Similar projects may require same stakeholders. Check lesson learned and register.
    - o **Analyze** all identified stakeholders to determine the following classifications:
        - Power/Interest grid with respect to their interest on the success of the project.
        - Power/Influence grid with respect to their influence or involvement in the project.
        - Influence/Impact grid with respect to having power to effect changes in planning or execution.

- Salience Model – stakeholders that have the power to impose their will, initiate urgency and with legitimate standing on the project.
  - Organize **meetings** with prospective stakeholders to determine their influence level. Collectively or individually.

- ❖ **Plan Stakeholders Management** - A planning process. It involves developing strategies for engaging stakeholders at different stages of project lifecycle based on their needs, influence, interest and impact on the success of the project.
  - The selected **project life cycle** is a key to planning how stakeholders will be engaged during the project.
  - The **sponsors and influencers** are needed actively at the beginning to clarify the scope of the project.
  - **Different roles,** responsibilities and requirements of human resources will be required at **different stages of the project**.
  - Changes introduced or requested by stakeholders must be documented and followed through a **change process** agreed by all affected parties. Effective communication.
  - Planning must include how status, risk and changes are **effectively communicated** to all stakeholders.
  - Expert judgment, history or previous lesson learned may be consulted to effectively plan stakeholders' engagement in the project.
    - Use the engagement level classification matrix approach:
      - Unaware – Unaware of the project
      - Resistant– Resistant to the project
      - Neutral – Indifferent on the project
      - Supportive – Supportive of the project
      - Leading – Engaged and actively pushing project success.

- ❖ **Manage Stakeholders Management.** This is the actual process of communicating and engaging the stakeholders during the project lifecycle. The stakeholders' expectations, needs and issues are addressed during this process while meeting the overall objectives of the project.

- o **Follow the strategies** laid out in plan for involving the stakeholders at different levels of the project phases.
- o Address stakeholders' communication requirements using the appropriate level of information distribution format:
    - Verbal – Formal or non-formal meetings
    - Documentation with appropriate templates
        - Email
        - Documents with detailed content and headings
        - Notes
- o Adhere to the escalation process of communication.
- o Apply Interpersonal skills to manage the stakeholders:
    - Manage conflict where necessary.
    - Overcome resistance to change by influence.
    - Build trust by following appropriate communication channel.
- o Apply management skills through
    - Facilitation of all required activities and stakeholders
    - Influencing people
    - Negotiation requirements and agreements
    - Modification of behavior for project success.

❖ **Control Stakeholder Engagement.** This is the process of monitoring stakeholder engagements and making adjustments in strategies and plans to control their involvement and overall relationships with the project.
- o Control the engagement of stakeholders by involving the respective parties at the relevant stage of the project lifecycle.
- o The works defined for the project should help in determine when relevant stakeholder is engaged in the project.
- o The roles and responsibilities, human resources requirement will have defined the respective stakeholders to be engaged in the project.
- o Control stakeholders' engagement using the relevant change process method monitor their change request

- and impact on the project outcome.
  - An issue log to track all issues reported should be in place.
  - Use the appropriate communication method to control information distribution to the stakeholders. This is important in minimizing noise in project information distribution.
  - Finally, document all changes introduced from stakeholders' engagement for traceability.

Chapter 20: PMI® Code of Ethics and Professional Conduct

This area of PMI® standard is an important aspect that differentiates project managers as professional and nonprofessionals. A professional approach is applied to all situations irrespective of the circumstance surrounding the situations. The requirement from PMI® standards is responsibility, respect, fairness, and honesty. My formula for memorizing this requirement is R^2FH. The following sections of this book are copied directly from the PMI® standard to avoid any misinterpretation and maintain accuracy as defined by the Project Management Institute.

Source: PMP® Handbook from PMI®

PMI® CHAPTER 1. VISION AND APPLICABILITY

1.1 Vision and Purpose

As practitioners of project management, we are committed to doing what is right and honorable. We set high standards for ourselves and we aspire to meet these standards in all aspects of our lives—at work, at home, and in service to our profession.

This Code of Ethics and Professional Conduct describes the expectations that we have of ourselves and our fellow practitioners in the global project management community. It articulates the ideals to which we aspire as well as the behaviors that are mandatory in our professional and volunteer roles.

The purpose of this Code is to instill confidence in the project management profession and to help an individual become a better practitioner. We do this by establishing a profession-wide understanding of appropriate behavior.

We believe that the credibility and reputation of the project management profession is shaped by the collective conduct of individual practitioners.

We believe that we can advance our profession, both individually and collectively, by embracing this Code of Ethics and Professional Conduct. We also believe that this Code will assist us in making wise decisions, particularly when faced with difficult situations where we may be asked to compromise our integrity or our values.

Our hope that this Code of Ethics and Professional Conduct will serve as a catalyst for others to study, deliberate, and write about ethics and values. Further, we hope that this Code will ultimately be used to build upon and evolve our profession.

1.2 Persons to Whom the Code Applies

The Code of Ethics and Professional Conduct applies to:
1.2.1 All PMI® members.

1.2.2 Individuals who are not members of PMI® but meet one or more of the following criteria:
1. Non-members who hold a PMI® certification
2. Non-members who apply to commence a PMI® certification process
3. Non-members who serve PMI® in a volunteer capacity.

Comment: *Those holding a Project Management Institute (PMI®®) credential (whether members or not) were previously held accountable to the Project*

Management Professional (PMP®®) or Certified Associate in Project Management (CAPM®) Code of Professional Conduct and continue to be held accountable to the PMI® Code of Ethics and Professional Conduct. In the past, PMI® also had separate ethics standards for members and for credentialed individuals. Stakeholders who contributed input to develop this Code concluded that having multiple codes was undesirable and that everyone should be held to one high standard. Therefore, this Code is applicable to both PMI® members and individuals who have applied for or received a credential from PMI®, regardless of their membership in PMI®.

1.3 Structure of the Code

The Code of Ethics and Professional Conduct is divided into sections that contain standards of conduct which are aligned with the four values that were identified as most important to the project management community. Some sections of this Code include comments. Comments are not mandatory parts of the Code, but provide examples and other clarification. Finally, a glossary can be found at the end of the standard. The glossary defines words and phrases used in the Code. For convenience, those terms defined in the glossary are underlined in the text of the Code.

1.4 Values that Support this Code

Practitioners from the global project management community were asked to identify the values that formed the basis of their decision making and guided their actions. The values that the global project management community defined as most important were: responsibility, respect, fairness, and honesty. This Code affirms these four values as its foundation.

1.5 Aspirational and Mandatory Conduct

Each section of the Code of Ethics and Professional Conduct includes both aspirational standards and mandatory standards. The aspirational standards describe the conduct that we strive to uphold as practitioners. Although adherence to the aspirational standards is not easily measured, conducting ourselves in accordance with these is an expectation that we have of ourselves as professionals—it is not optional. The mandatory standards establish firm requirements, and in some cases, limit or prohibit practitioner behavior. Practitioners who do not conduct themselves in accordance with these standards will be subject to disciplinary procedures before PMI®'s Ethics Review Committee.

Comment: *The conduct covered under the aspirational standards and conduct covered under the mandatory standards are not mutually exclusive; that is, one specific act or omission could violate both aspirational and mandatory standards.*

PMI® CHAPTER 2. RESPONSIBILITY

2.1 Description of Responsibility

Responsibility is our duty to take ownership for the decisions we make or fail to make, the actions we take or fail to take, and the consequences that result.

2.2 Responsibility: Aspirational Standards

As practitioners in the global project management community:
2.2.1 We make decisions and take actions based on the best interests of society, public safety, and the environment.
2.2.2 We accept only those assignments that are consistent with our background, experience, skills, and qualifications.

Comment: *Where developmental or stretch assignments are being considered, we ensure that key stakeholders receive timely and complete information regarding the gaps in our qualifications so that they may make informed decisions regarding our suitability for a particular assignment. In the case of a contracting arrangement, we only bid on work that our organization is qualified* *to perform and we assign only qualified individuals to perform the work.*

2.2.3   We fulfill the commitments that we undertake—we do what we say we will do.

2.2.4   When we make errors or omissions, we take ownership and make corrections promptly. When we discover errors or omissions caused by others, we communicate them to the appropriate body as soon they are discovered. We accept accountability for any issues resulting from our errors or omissions and any resulting consequences.

2.2.5   We protect proprietary or confidential information that has been entrusted to us.

2.2.6   We uphold this Code and hold each other accountable to it.

2.3 Responsibility: Mandatory Standards

As practitioners in the global project management community, we require the following of ourselves and our fellow practitioners:
Regulations and Legal Requirements

2.3.1.   We inform ourselves and uphold the policies, rules, regulations and laws that govern our work, professional, and volunteer activities.
2.3.2.   We report unethical or illegal conduct to appropriate management and, if necessary, to those affected by the conduct.

Comment: *These provisions have several implications. Specifically, we do not engage in any illegal behavior, including but not limited to: theft, fraud, corruption, embezzlement, or bribery. Further, we do not take or abuse the property of others, including intellectual property, nor do we engage in slander or libel. In focus groups conducted with practitioners around the globe, these types of illegal behaviors were mentioned as being problematic. As practitioners and representatives of our profession, we do not condone or assist others in engaging in illegal behavior. We report any illegal or unethical conduct. Reporting is not easy and we recognize that* it may have negative consequences. *Since recent corporate scandals, many organizations have adopted policies to protect employees who reveal the truth about illegal or unethical activities. Some governments have also adopted legislation to protect employees who come forward with the truth.*

Ethics Complaints

2.3.3. We bring violations of this Code to the attention of the appropriate body for resolution.

2.3.4. We only file ethics complaints when they are substantiated by facts.

Comment: *These provisions have several implications. We cooperate with PMI® concerning ethics violations and the collection of related information whether we are a complainant or a respondent. We also abstain from accusing others of ethical misconduct when we do not have all the facts. Further, we pursue disciplinary action against individuals who knowingly make false allegations against others.*

2.3.5. We pursue disciplinary action against an individual who retaliates against a person raising ethics concerns.

PMI® CHAPTER 3. RESPECT

3.1 Description of Respect

Respect is our duty to show a high regard for ourselves, others, and the resources entrusted to us. Resources entrusted to us may include people, money, reputation, the safety of others, and natural or environmental resources.

An environment of respect engenders trust, confidence, and performance excellence by fostering mutual cooperation—an environment where diverse perspectives and views are encouraged and valued.

3.2 Respect: Aspirational Standards

As practitioners in the global project management community:

3.2.1. We inform ourselves about the norms and customs of others and avoid engaging in behaviors they might consider disrespectful.
3.2.2. We listen to others' points of view, seeking to understand them.
3.2.3. We approach directly those persons with whom we have a conflict or disagreement.
3.2.4. We conduct ourselves in a professional manner, even when it is not reciprocated.

Comment: *An implication of these provisions is that we avoid engaging in gossip and avoid making negative remarks to undermine another person's reputation. We also have a duty under this Code to confront others who engage in these types of behaviors.*

3.3 Respect: Mandatory Standards

As practitioners in the global project management community, we require the following of ourselves and our fellow practitioners:

3.3.1. We negotiate in good faith.
3.3.2. We do not exercise the power of our expertise or position to influence the decisions or actions of others in order to benefit personally at their expense.
3.3.3. We do not act in an abusive manner toward others.
3.3.4. We respect the property rights of others.

PMI® CHAPTER 4. FAIRNESS

4.1 Description of Fairness

Fairness is our duty to make decisions and act impartially and objectively. Our conduct must be free from competing self interest, prejudice, and favoritism.

4.2 Fairness: Aspirational Standards

As practitioners in the global project management community:
4.2.1. We demonstrate transparency in our decision-making

process.

4.2.2. We constantly reexamine our impartiality and objectivity, taking corrective action as appropriate.

Comment: *Research with practitioners indicated that the subject of conflicts of interest is one of the most challenging faced by our profession. One of the biggest problems practitioners report is not recognizing when we have conflicted loyalties and recognizing when we are inadvertently placing ourselves or others in a conflict of interest situation. We as practitioners must proactively search for potential conflicts and help each other by highlighting each other's potential conflicts of interest and insisting that they be resolved.*

4.2.3. We provide equal access to information to those who are authorized to have that information.

4.2.4. We make opportunities equally available to qualified candidates.

Comment: *An implication of these provisions is, in the case of a contracting arrangement, we provide equal access to information during the bidding process.*

4.3 Fairness: Mandatory Standards

As practitioners in the global project management community, we require the following of ourselves and our fellow practitioners:

Conflict of Interest Situations

4.3.1. We proactively and fully disclose any real or potential conflicts of interest to the appropriate stakeholders.

4.3.2. When we realize that we have a real or potential conflict of interest, we refrain from engaging in the decision-making process or otherwise attempting to influence outcomes, unless or until: we have made full disclosure to the affected stakeholders; we have an approved mitigation plan; and we have obtained the consent of the stakeholders to proceed.

Comment: *A conflict of interest occurs when we are in a position to influence decisions or other outcomes on behalf of one party when such decisions or outcomes could affect one or more other parties with which we have competing loyalties. For example, when we are acting as an employee, we have a duty of loyalty to our employer. When we are acting as a PMI® volunteer, we have a duty of loyalty to the Project Management Institute. We must recognize these divergent interests and refrain from influencing decisions when we have a conflict of interest.*

Further, even if we believe that we can set aside our divided loyalties and make decisions impartially, we treat the appearance of a conflict of interest as a conflict of interest and follow the provisions described in the Code.

Favoritism and Discrimination

4.3.3. We do not hire or fire, reward or punish, or award or deny contracts based on personal considerations, including but not limited to, favoritism, nepotism, or bribery.

4.3.4. We do not discriminate against others based on, but not limited to, gender, race, age, religion, disability, nationality, or sexual orientation.

4.3.5. We apply the rules of the organization (employer, Project Management Institute, or other group) without favoritism or prejudice.

PMI® CHAPTER 5. HONESTY

5.1 Description of Honesty

Honesty is our duty to understand the truth and act in a truthful manner both in our communications and in our conduct.

5.2 Honesty: Aspirational Standards

As practitioners in the global project management community:

5.2.1. We earnestly seek to understand the truth.

5.2.2. We are truthful in our communications and in our conduct.

5.2.3. We provide accurate information in a timely manner.

Comment: *An implication of these provisions is that we take appropriate steps to ensure that the information we are basing our decisions upon or providing to others is accurate, reliable, and timely. This includes having the courage to share bad news even when it may be poorly received. Also, when outcomes are negative, we avoid burying information or shifting blame to others. When outcomes are positive, we avoid taking credit for the achievements of others. These provisions reinforce our commitment to be both honest and responsible.*

5.2.4. We make commitments and promises, implied or explicit, in good faith.

5.2.5. We strive to create an environment in which others feel safe to tell the truth.

5.3 Honesty: Mandatory Standards

As practitioners in the global project management community, we require the following of ourselves and our fellow practitioners:

5.3.1. We do not engage in or condone behavior that is designed to deceive others, including but not limited to, making misleading or false statements, stating half-truths, providing information out of context or withholding information that, if known, would render our statements as misleading or incomplete.

5.3.2. We do not engage in dishonest behavior with the intention of personal gain or at the expense of another.

Comment: *The aspirational standards exhort us to be truthful. Half-truths and non-disclosures intended to mislead stakeholders are as unprofessional as affirmatively making misrepresentations. We develop credibility by providing complete and accurate information.*

Appendix A

A.1 History of this Standard

PMI®'s vision of project management as an independent profession drove our early work in ethics. In 1981, the PMI® Board of Directors formed an Ethics, Standards and Accreditation Group. One task required the group to deliberate on the need for a code of ethics for the profession. The team's report contained the first documented PMI® discussion of ethics for the project management profession. This report was submitted to the PMI® Board of Directors in August 1982 and published as a supplement to the August 1983 Project Management Quarterly.

In the late 1980's, this standard evolved to become the Ethics Standard for the Project Management Professional [PMP®®]. In 1997, the PMI® Board determined the need for a member code of ethics. The PMI® Board formed the Ethics Policy Documentation Committee to draft and publish an ethics standard for PMI®'s membership. The Board approved the new Member Code of Ethics in October 1998. This was followed by Board approval of the Member Case Procedures in January 1999, which provided a process for the submission of an ethics complaint and a determination as to whether a violation had occurred.

Since the 1998 Code was adopted, many dramatic changes have occurred within PMI® and the business world. PMI® membership has grown significantly. A great deal of growth has also occurred in regions outside North America. In the business world, ethics scandals have caused the downfall global corporations and non-profits, causing public outrage and sparking increased government regulations. Globalization has brought economies closer together but has caused a realization that our practice of ethics may differ from culture to culture. The rapid, continuing pace of technological change has provided new opportunities, but has also introduced new challenges, including new ethical dilemmas.

For these reasons, in 2003 the PMI® Board of Directors called for the reexamination of our codes of ethics. In 2004, the PMI® Board commissioned the Ethics Standards Review Committee [ESRC] to review the codes of ethics and develop a process for revising the codes. The ESRC developed processes that would encourage active participation by the global project management community. In 2005, the PMI® Board approved the processes for revising the code, agreeing that global participation by the project management community was paramount. In 2005, the Board also commissioned the Ethics Standards Development Committee to carry out the Board-approved process and deliver the revised code by the end of 2006. This Code of Ethics and Professional Development was approved by the PMI® Board of Directors in October 2006.

A.2 Process Used to Create This Standard

The first step by the Ethics Standards Development Committee [ESDC] in the development of this Code was to understand the ethical issues facing the project management community and to understand the values and viewpoints of practitioners from all regions of the globe. This was accomplished by a variety of mechanisms including focus group discussions and two internet surveys involving practitioners, members, volunteers, and people holding a PMI® certification. Additionally, the team analyzed the ethics codes of 24 non-profit associations from various regions of the world, researched best practices in the development of ethics standards, and explored the ethics-related tenets of PMI®'s strategic plan.

This extensive research conducted by the ESDC provided the backdrop for developing the exposure draft of the PMI® Code of Ethics and Professional Conduct. The exposure draft was circulated to the global project management community for comment. The rigorous, standards development processes established by the American National Standards Institute were followed during the development of the Code because these processes were used for PMI® technical standard development projects and were deemed to represent the best practices for obtaining and adjudicating stakeholder feedback to the exposure draft.

The result of this effort is a Code of Ethics and Professional Conduct that not only describes the ethical values to which the global project management community aspires, but also addresses the specific conduct that is mandatory for every individual bound by this Code. Violations of the PMI® Code of Ethics and Professional Conduct may result in sanctions by PMI® under the ethics Case Procedures.

The ESDC learned that as practitioners of project management, our community takes its commitment to ethics very seriously and we hold ourselves and our peers in the global project management community accountable to conduct ourselves in accordance with the provisions of this Code.

Appendix B

B.1 Glossary

Abusive Manner. Conduct that results in physical harm or creates intense feelings of fear, humiliation, manipulation, or exploitation in another person.

Conflict of Interest. A situation that arises when a practitioner of project management is faced with making a decision or doing some act that will benefit the practitioner or another person or organization to which the practitioner owes a duty of loyalty and at the same time will harm another person or organization to which the practitioner owes a similar duty of loyalty. The only way practitioners can resolve conflicting duties is to disclose the conflict to those affected and allow them to make the decision about how the practitioner should proceed.

Duty of Loyalty. A person's responsibility, legal or moral, to promote the best interest of an organization or other person with whom they are affiliated.

Project Management Institute [PMI®]. The totality of the Project Management Institute, including it's

Committees, groups, and chartered components such as chapters, colleges, and specific interest groups.

PMI® Member. A person who has joined the Project Management Institute as a member.

PMI®-Sponsored Activities. Activities that include, but are not limited to, participation on a PMI® Member Advisory Group, PMI® standard development team, or another PMI® working group or committee. This also includes activities engaged in under the auspices of a chartered PMI® component organization—whether it is in a leadership role in the component or another type of component educational activity or event.

Practitioner. A person engaged in an activity that contributes to the management of a project, portfolio, or program, as part of the project management profession.

PMI® Volunteer. A person who participates in PMI®-sponsored activities, whether a member of the Project Management Institute or not.

About the Author

David London, BEng (Hons), MEng (Hons), MIEE, PMP®, from Coventry University, UK, is a principal consultant with big five consulting companies. He consulted for several Fortune 1000 clients worldwide including American Management Systems, UK; Capgemini; Ernst & Young, USA; Convergys, USA; SiriusXM, USA Brown & Sharpe, UK; and British Gas, and now with AITechConsulting Ltd.

His experience includes business, engineering, and IT consultation for major corporations in countries including Great Britain, France, Spain, Germany, Switzerland, Saudi Arabia, and the USA. His experience in project and program management included project management of multidisciplinary large-scale billing and operation support systems for telecom, transportation, retail, financial, and manufacturing industries.

AITECHCONSULTING LLC, USA.

PO Box 1213
Laurel, MD, 20725, USA
Attention: General Counsel
Phone: 1800 561 02 63
E-mail: businessdev@aitechconsulting.com
Website: www.aitechconsulting.com

www.ingramcontent.com/pod-product-compliance
Lightning Source LLC
Chambersburg PA
CBHW071550220526
45469CB00003B/963